Assemblies

for liturgical seas
& school occasio

Volume 1

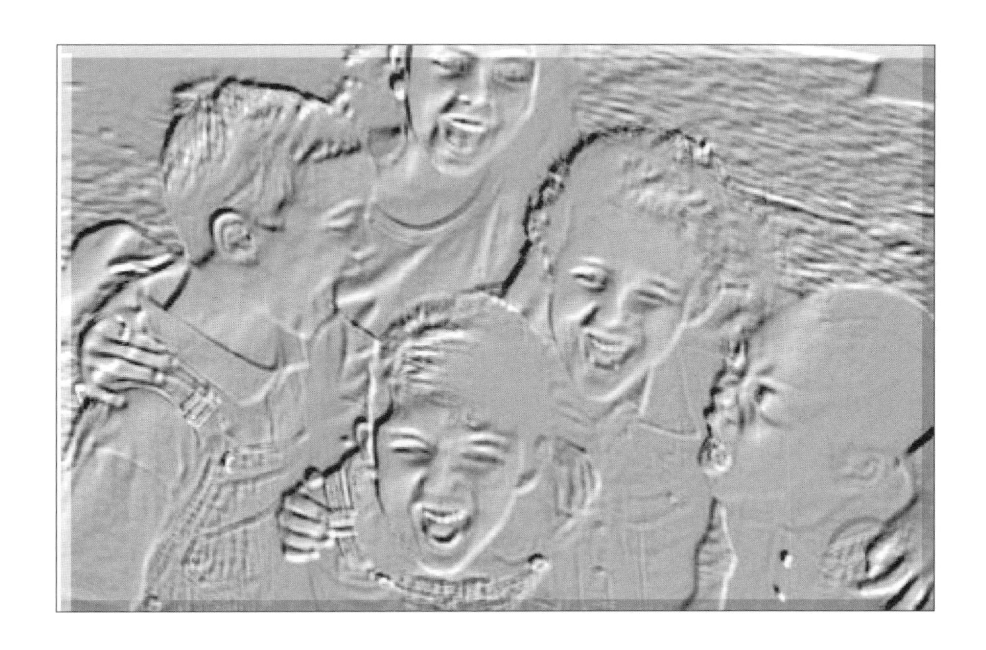

Jude Groden RSM

Christopher O'Donnell O.CARM

McCRIMMONS
Great Wakering, Essex, England

The images used inside this book are available on CD:

Religious Clip Art on CD – Omnibus Edition	Ref: COCDP
Signs, Symbols & Saints	Ref: SSSCD

First published in 1999 by
McCrimmon Publishing Co. Ltd.
10-12 High Street, Great Wakering, Essex SS3 0EQ
Telephone 01702–218956
Fax 01702–216082
Email: mccrimmons@dial.pipex.com
Web site: www.mccrimmons.co.uk

ISBN 0 85597 615 2

Illustrations by The Benedictine Sisters of Turvey Abbey
Page 79: illustration by Peter Edwards

Cover design and page layout: Nick Snode
Typeset in Revival 12pt roman and Frutiger 11/13pt roman
Printed by Black Bear Press Ltd, Cambridge

I/II

Contents

Preface 5
Introduction – School Worship 6

Seasons

Advent 1	*The time is at hand*	12
Advent 2	*John the Baptist*	14
Advent 3	*Mary*	16
Advent 4	*Just before Christmas*	18
Lent 1	*The Season*	20
Lent 2	*Giving things up*	22
Lent 3	*Taking things up*	24
Lent 4	*Going apart to the mountain of God*	26
Lent 5	*The poor*	28
Lent 6	*The Bethany visit*	30
Lent 7	*The King comes to Jerusalem*	32
Lent 8	*The Last Supper*	34
Lent 9	*Good Friday*	36
Easter 1	*The Resurrection*	38
Easter 2	*Life*	40
Easter 3	*The Risen Lord*	42
Easter 4	*Joy*	44
Easter	*Ascension*	46
Pentecost 1	*The Holy Spirit*	48
Pentecost 2	*Wisdom*	50
Pentecost 3	*Reverence*	52
Pentecost 4	*Love*	54

Pentecost 5 — *Peace* 56
Ordinary Time — *Corpus Christi* 58
Ordinary Time — *The Holy Trinity* 60

School occasions

First Communion 62
Opening of the school year 64
Closing of the school year 66
Welcome to a new teacher or staff member 68
Retirement of a teacher or staff member 70
Harvest thanksgiving 72
Inspection time 74
Examination time 76
Remembrance 78
Christian unity 80
Election time 84
Anniversary of school's foundation 86
Ethnic celebrations 88
School outing – journeys 90
Death of a pupil 92
Death of a teacher / staff member / friend of school 94
National grief 96
A time of tragedy 98
Reconciliation 100

Brentwood Religious Education Service

Cathedral House,
Ingrave Road, Brentwood,
Essex. CM15 8AT

Telephone:
Brentwood (01277) 215689
Fax: (01277) 214060

The most important part of the school day in a Catholic school is the Collective Act of Worship. It orientates the school to it's mission, which is to educate children in and for a world made by God. It helps children and staff to focus on the central reason for the school being in existence – God. the original teacher and carer of humanity.

Most schools find themselves under pressure in providing stimulating material to help and encourage prayer and spiritual growth. Teachers have such a wealth of responsibilities to meet – literacy and numeracy hours, adequate information and communication technology training, lesson preparation and marking – that, from time to time, they are faced with an assembly and little time to prepare. Here is a resource which provides a structured progression to develop the sense of the presence of God, a training in prayer and development of spirituality for children up to keystage 3.

Those who have written and compiled this resource rely on their experience as teachers and experts in practical theology as suitable for growing young minds and hearts. However, children learn from the lived experience of those who teach them directly on a day-to-day basis. It is to be hoped that this resource will enhance the prayer-experience, not only of the pupils, but also of the teachers, whose spiritual development impinges so forcefully on the lives of their charges.

Fr. George Stokes

Director of Education
Diocese of Brentwood

School Worship

The School Assembly is both opportunity and challenge. For some schools it is a legal demand, one indeed open to many interpretations within the Education Reform Act (1988), which specifies that school worship is to be both religious and educational. Whilst few perhaps will doubt the potential of school assemblies and worship, many practical problems emerge from day to day. There are issues of content and approach to such worship; not all in the school will see it the same way, value it similarly, or engage in it with the same commitment. There are difficulties about guiding such worship and the ages and aptitudes of those participating. There is surely a problem from the very regularity of school worship: few people can be continually creative; constant innovation may be detrimental to the religious and educational aims of worship; sameness can lead to a stultifying monotony.

There is surely no one approach to school worship. Even within a Christian or more particularly a Catholic ethos, there are very many legitimate ways of communal worship that answer the guidelines given by educational authorities. The present volume seeks to help schools with worship drawing on contemporary insights about spirituality and doctrines in a way that would be helpful in both a religious and an educational perspective. Other models of assembly will have their place too. This book of assemblies along with the a second being prepared, offers teachers an outline that may either be followed quite closely, or better still, used as a framework within mainly primary and lower secondary schools. Trial use of these assemblies in various schools over the past year showed that the approach and content were helpful to hard-pressed teachers.

Aims of school worship

Even within the broad aims of school worship as religious and educational, there are many interpretations and possibilities. An earlier generation would perhaps have seen worship as self-justifying, something that the Christian would want to do, and which needs no further apology. Our age is more pragmatic and result conscious, and poses the question, what use is school worship? An immediate answer might be to say that an education that looks to the whole person cannot neglect a spiritual dimension of the individual and of the school itself. The frequently quoted DFE Circular 1/94, § 50 gives a number of aims that indicate possibilities of worship for the life of pupils and the school:

"Collective worship in schools should aim…

- to provide the opportunity for pupils to worship God
- to consider spiritual and moral issues
- to explore their own beliefs
- to encourage participation and response whether through active

involvement in the presentation of worship or through listening to and joining in the worship offered
- to develop community spirit
- to promote a common ethos and shared values
- to reinforce positive attitudes."

These aims can be seen to reflect an important teaching of the Second Vatican Council, "One of the gravest errors of our time is the dichotomy between the faith which many profess and their day-to-day conduct." (*Church in the Modern World*, GS 43)
One way of avoiding such a division between faith and daily life is to seek to integrate life and worship. Our daily lives lead into worship; our worship must flow over into our lives. It is helped when one can find a religious perspective for the concerns of daily life, and show that the affairs of daily life are not alien to religion and worship. The assemblies in this volume attempt just such integration and in so doing would wish to work for the aims in the DEF Circular.

Features of school assemblies

The structure and elements of the school assemblies in this work stress some important features of school worship and might be seen as answering the aims given above.

1 Entrance music (tape or CD)

It is suggested that when pupils come to assembly that there be some suitable background music being played. This will help to set the atmosphere for the worship, which is to follow. It helps the pupils to realise that in some way the worship time is special, set apart from the other activities of the school day. Though God is everywhere present in supporting creation, there is a special presence of Christ in the reading of scripture and in the prayer and singing of those who gather in his name (see Vatican II, *Liturgy*, SC 7).

2 Introduction

Each assembly has a suggested introduction. Teachers will of course often want to supply their own introduction. The models provided here seek to give the theme of the celebration, to say why we are today gathering in worship. Already the Introduction gives the possibility of relating the life of the pupils or the school both to the worship of God and to the world around them.

3 Focus or symbol

The use of a focus or symbol helps to bring out the theme of the celebration. It is a centre of attention. The focus or symbol is yet another way in which school worship is a transfer to sacred time or space, yet within the practicalities of ordinary life.

Various suggestions are made that schools will wish to modify. An overhead projector can be a convenient way of drawing attention to a word, phrase, or symbol. For special occasions more attention can be given to providing a symbol or focus, but for regular school worship it will not be possible to provide a stimulating symbol for every day.

A question can arise about explaining symbols. Symbols are generally open, and can be entered into at various levels: a flag or poster will move people differently. Though it is sometimes helpful to draw people's attention to a symbol, detailed explanations can kill a symbol. The explanation restricts the meaning that others will take from it; the power of the symbol is cut off by words. People can share in a symbol without understanding it or how it operates. Indeed it would be better to say that symbols do not so much explain as open up meaning. A picture of a dove on an overhead can allow people to enter into the quiet of the dove, its freedom, its lightness, and its simple beauty. Such feelings – and symbols operate primarily at the level of feeling – could be cut off by telling the pupils too much about doves.

One cannot be absolute in this matter. Younger pupils can be helped to enter into the world of symbols, in which anyway they are already operating. But in general for older pupils, a good symbol does not need too much explanation. We draw attention to it and let it speak to the individual.

4 Sign of the Cross

Catholic prayer usually begins with the Sign of the Cross, "In the name of the Father and of the Son and of the Holy Spirit. Amen." This invocation is an entering into prayer. The brief introduction provides a transition from the Introduction to actual prayer.

5 Hymn or song

Opinions will vary about the best place for hymns. If they are placed at the very beginning pupils may not be sufficiently attentive or alert, and the meaning can be lost. The hymn is a way in which pupils can actively take part in the worship of the assembly. At times a taped hymn may be used, especially when a hymn or song is not yet familiar, but in general it would seem to be better to have the pupils sing rather than to listen to a song. There are two extremes to be avoided: over frequent use of the same hymn can lead to monotony in hymns, and people grow tired even of favourite ones. But on the other hand a school repertoire can only be built up slowly. The hymns given for the assemblies in this book are only examples of what might be appropriate for a particular celebration.

6 Reading

The readings in these assemblies are usually from scripture. There is no reason why other readings cannot be used. But some care needs to be taken that the reading does lead to the double focus of school worship, namely being religious and educational. In the last few decades the Catholic Church has given ever-increasing attention to scripture as the source of its life and its worship. In the scriptures we hear God's word that lifts us up, instructs us, corrects us, trains us in holiness (see 2 Tim 3:16-17).

Moreover the reading is yet another example of how the life of the school radiates outwards and upwards. The scripture draws our attention to the need to be serving and loving in our school, family and society; it also reminds us of God's loving providence which surrounds us and continually leads us to God and the great mysteries.

7 Comment on reading

As in the case of symbols we have to avoid being too clear-cut in explanations of the readings. But they are not self-evident and we can always be enriched by the insights of another into a passage, even one that we think we already thoroughly know. The living faith of teachers who meet with God's word and then share in a simple way what this word means to them is a powerful witness. The comments in this book are merely suggestive about ways in which the scripture text can be integrated into the act of the worship, and the lives of the pupils and teachers.

8 Response to reading

Prayer and worship are a dialogue. We hear God's word, we consider a special theme. We cannot leave it there. Some response is called for. The responses ideally should grow from the whole worship. It can be a phrase, a gesture, or a movement. It may be a silent prayer, but in this last case it would be good to indicate at least in general the direction which this prayer might take, e.g. think of something that you might give thanks for/somebody whom you should forgive… Though there are suggestions supplied for the busy teacher, this response phase is one in which there can be great creativity.

9 Prayers

The format chosen for the prayers has been that of invitation and response. The invitations to pray opens up vast possibilities. Here there can be a profound blending of the religious and educational dimensions of worship. Praying teaches us how to pray. They indicate ways in which we can approach God, consider our world, and look at our needs. The prayers in this volume seek to open up the awareness of pupils to the needs in the society (the marginalised, the sick, and those in special difficulties). But they also seek to show that Christian prayer should look at our whole society and bring all of it before God. Thus there is an attempt to alert pupils and teachers to the many people who make a contribution to our society, for example workers in manufacturing areas, farmers, civil administrators, voluntary bodies, state, economic and political institutions etc. Many prayers open up to needs beyond the shores of our country to the work of international agencies like the Red Cross/Crescent, CAFOD, UNESCO, UN Peacekeeping Forces, and missionaries. Pupils are invited to bring their own joys and sorrows to worship, but at the same time to look beyond their own needs to that of others.

Again, the prayers are suggestions, and there is a suggestion that each worship period should have other prayers added which correspond to particular issues in the school, the neighbourhood, or events in the news that call Christians to pray and to intercede.

10 Thought-Word-Phrase for the Day

The period of worship is a highpoint of the day. It cannot remain isolated, and should carry over into the rest of the day. One way to help this process is the selection of a thought, word or phrase that is given to the assembly at the end that sums up or focuses what has been celebrated. One should not underestimate the possibilities of such a phrase. We are all familiar with the power of advertising and the way in which its subliminal messages fashion our attitudes towards particular products or services. We are the same creatures of mind and body that are influenced by secular advertising as well also by Christian thoughts. The worship with its readings, symbols, prayers and ideas will gradually transform us. The use of a Thought-Word-Phrase for the day is one way in which the school communicates values. The ones given in this volume are of course only suggestions. Were other teachers to refer occasionally to the Thought-Word-Phrase at some later time, then there would be possibilities for still deeper integration of worship and life.

11 Blessing

In the past blessings were almost exclusively associated with ordained ministers, and indeed some blessings are still their special competence. But the rediscovery of Celtic spirituality in these islands has alerted us to a profound theme in Christian life, as seen especially by the Celtic peoples in our society. A very common greeting in Celtic languages such as Welsh, Scots Gaelic and Irish was a blessing, "God bless all here," "God bless the work," "Praise God for a beautiful day."

Blessing in scripture had a double meaning. It was something that we received from God; it is a bringing before God of people, circumstances and things. Such blessings are often expressed as a wish or a prayer directed to God. The blessings in this volume are again only indicative of the sort of conclusion that the worship might have.

Some biblical blessings are used frequently to make them familiar, such as Numbers 6:24-26 and 2 Corinthians 13:13. These are used extensively by various Christian bodies as blessings, and in Catholic worship the latter is used as a liturgical greeting.

From a liturgical point of view one might state that in using these blessings the leader of the assembly and all present could make the sign of the Cross on themselves. It is not appropriate for one who is not a deacon or priest to impose hands over the assembly or to make the sign of the Cross over them, as an official act of blessing during liturgical worship.

12 Concluding song or music

The concluding music may be a hymn sung by all, it may also be music already recorded. Its aim is to create a bridge of transition back to other school realities.

Key for hymnbooks

CFE	=	Celebration Hymnal for Everyone
O&N	=	Hymns Old & New

THE TWO VOLUMES

The two volumes offered to teachers seek to combine the skills and expertise of a teacher and of a theologian in providing assemblies that are rich doctrinally and educationally sound. The first volume offers assemblies for the special seasons of Advent, Lent, Eastertide and Pentecost as well as assemblies for special occasions in the life of a school community. The second volume will provide assemblies based on Christian feasts of the Virgin Mary and of the saints. The lives of the saints have been described as living commentaries on the gospel. They open up new possibilities for Christian living and as a continual source of encouragement and upbuilding. At the same time attention to various saints both contemporary and older, as well as saints from particular national or ethnic backgrounds allow people to enter into the fullness of the Communion of Saints, the sharing that takes place between God's people on earth and in glory.

TEACH US TO PRAY

Prayer has to be learned. But the teaching is not merely by instruction. The great teacher of prayer is the Holy Spirit who has been poured out into our hearts (see Rom 5:5). It is the Spirit who forms our lives and also our prayer (see Rom 8:26-27). We can learn prayers, we can learn forms of prayer from others. There is, however, always more. Prayer builds a relationship with God, so that the Christian mysteries are brought into our lives and made meaningful for us. Without prayer religious instruction will be a matter for the head alone. With prayer we can make our own the values and realities that are taught in the community and by the Church. Through prayer we find and reflect on the things that make our lives meaningful and enriched. The relationship established by prayer is not merely with God. Because we bring others and the full scope of our lives into prayer, it builds relationships with others. It is hard to be continually angry with somebody for whom we pray frequently – we will either forgive, or give up praying for the person; consideration of the teaching of Jesus should influence our dealings with others – prayer purifies our hearts and moulds our behaviour. Prayer then forms relationships with God and with others. It has therefore a continuing role in the development of the person. And as the person develops, so too should prayer, so that the gospel petition "teach us to pray" (Luke 11:1) will be life-long as we continue to learn the ways of worship and prayer, building relationships ever more deeply with God and with others and being changed and healed in the process (see *Catechism of the Catholic Church*, part IV).

The time is at hand

1 Entrance music (tape or CD) Choose a suitable piece of music

2 Introduction

We are all used to different years: the football year starts in August; the civil year starts in January; the cricket year starts in April. The Church's year starts at the beginning of December. The four weeks or so that come before Christmas are a time of preparation, when we think of Jesus coming into the world. We also think of his coming into our lives and of his Second Coming at the end of the world.

3 Focus or symbol

- Advent wreath

  and/or

- Advent banner with the words:

  'Come, Lord Jesus'
  or
  'The Time is at hand.'

4 Sign of the Cross

The core of our faith is the Trinity, – God the Father, God the Son and God the Holy Spirit. God sent His Son to be born and to die for us. So we begin, "In the name of the Father and of the Son and of the Holy Spirit."

5 Hymn or song

CFE		O&N
366	Light the Advent Candle One	
368	Like a sea without a shore	311
S10	Christ be our Light	
	Come Lord Jesus	684

6 Reading *Matthew 24: 42-44*

Be on your guard then because you do not know what day the Lord will come. Stay awake! You also must always be ready because the Son of Man will come at an hour when you were not expecting him.

7 Comment on reading

At the time of Jesus people were watching for the Messiah to come. When he, Jesus, came they did not recognise him. Jesus came, but Jesus is also coming. He comes in various ways. He comes through grace into our lives; he comes in the needs of others; he comes when we receive love; he comes when we show love. A very important coming is when he comes to take us with him to heaven, when he comes at our death. There is also a coming at the end of the world. Some people are always wondering about the end of the world. In the years immediately before and after the millennium, there were dozens of forecasts about when Jesus would come and the world would end. And we are still here. Jesus is saying to us that we should not be calculating the time, but we should be ready: ready when his grace comes, ready in the needs of others, ready to celebrate Christmas, ready to welcome him when he comes to bring us to himself.

8 Response to Reading

A pupil carries an empty crib, which has straw and animals, but no human figures; or a pupil puts straw and animals into an otherwise empty crib.

10 Thought-Word-Phrase for the day

'Emmanuel'

which means 'God is with us.'

9 Prayers

We pray for the needs of others and ourselves.

[a] For all people that they may discover the true meaning of Christmas, that is, God is with us.

Response: **Come, Lord Jesus; come to us in love.**

[b] For all who work to spread the good news that God is our loving Father, that Jesus is our Brother and that the Holy Spirit is our Helper and Guide.

Response: **Come, Lord Jesus; come to us in love.**

[c] For all who are trapped in the darkness of anger, and find it hard to for give.

Response: **Come, Lord Jesus; come to us in love.**

[d] For ourselves that we may have a love for the Word of God in the Bible.

Response: **Come, Lord Jesus; come to us in love.**

[e] For ourselves that we may prepare our hearts well for the coming of Jesus each day into our lives and at Christmas.

Response: **Come, Lord Jesus; come to us in love.**

[f] [other prayers]

Response: **Come, Lord Jesus; come to us in love.**

[g] Our Father (perhaps sung

11 Blessing

May God make us strong in faith,
joyful in hope,
and untiring in love
all our days.
Amen.

12 Concluding song or music

CFE		*O&N*
65	Awake from your slumber	
268	How lovely on the mountains	223/4
	Word made flesh, Son of God	619

John the Baptist

1 Entrance music (tape or CD)
Choose a suitable piece of music

2 Introduction

John the Baptist wanted people to see who Jesus was and to welcome him. But in order to recognise Jesus and meet him John urged people to change their lives and turn away from sin and selfishness. Jesus wants to come to us; we should try and remove obstacles to his love.

3 Focus or symbol

- Advent wreath
- Poster with desert scene
  Caption; *"Prepare the way of the Lord."*

4 Sign of the Cross

The Cross is a constant reminder to change our lives and prepare to live more closely with Jesus, and so we begin, "In the name of the Father and of the Son and of the Holy Spirit."

5 Hymn or Song

CFE		*O&N*
401	Water of Life	
612	Prepare ye the way of the Lord	
716	The Spirit of the Lord	548

6 Reading

Matthew 3:1-3

John the Baptist came to the desert of Judea and started preaching. "Turn away from your sins," he said, "because the Kingdom of heaven is near!" John was the man the prophet Isaiah was talking about when he said, "Someone is shouting in the desert, 'prepare a way for the Lord; make a straight path for him to travel'."

7 Comment on reading

Two figures dominate the Advent season, John the Baptist and Mary. During the first part of Lent we look to the figure of John. He was sent to prepare people's hearts for the coming of Jesus. He told them to turn away from sin, to live good lives. He does not point to himself but to Jesus. When sinners came he received them with kindness, even great sinners, provided they wanted to repent. But he had hard words for those who were not sincere. A key idea for Advent is repentance. But this is not a sad message: sin is bad for us; repentance brings us into life and peace.

8 Response to reading

In the silence of our hearts we reflect on ways that will prepare our hearts for the coming of Jesus.

[Silent pause]

10 Thought-Word-Phrase for the Day

Prepare for the Lord's coming

9 Prayers

Let us listen to the call of John the Baptist to change and prepare a way for the Lord as we pray.

[a] That all Christians may love you more.
Response: **Prepare for the coming of our Lord.**

[b] That all countries that are divided may be reconciled.
Response: **Prepare for the coming of our Lord.**

[c] That people may be generous and look after the poor always.
Response: **Prepare for the coming of our Lord.**

[d] That all who are alone at this time may be touched by your love.
Response: **Prepare for the coming of our Lord.**

[e] That we may open our hearts to Jesus and to others.
Response: **Prepare for the coming of our Lord.**

[f] [other prayers]
Response: **Prepare for the coming of our Lord.**

[g] Our Father (perhaps sung)

11 Blessing

May the blessing of our loving God come upon us this day; may we prepare to meet him and feel the presence and power of his Spirit always. Amen.

12 Concluding song or music

CFE		*O&N*
65	Awake from your slumber	
368	Like a sea without a shore (vv. 1 & 2)	311

Mary

1 Entrance music (tape or CD) Choose a suitable piece of music

2 Introduction

Advent has a double message. Firstly, it calls us to prepare for Christmas and secondly it reminds us to prepare for our final meeting with Jesus. We are not alone in these preparations. Mary is our Mother and the Mother of Jesus. She can show us Jesus.

3 Focus or symbol

- Advent wreath.
- Image of Mary
- Caption: *"Jesus show us your Mother: Mary show us your Son"*

4 Sign of the Cross

The Cross reminds us of God's immense love for us which was greater than death itself. So we begin "In the name of the Father and of the Son and of the Holy Spirit."

5 Hymn or song

CFE		O&N
187	From heaven you came (The Servant King)	
263	Holy Virgin by God's decree	218
831	You shall go out with joy	

6 Reading *Luke 1:28-38 (extracts)*

The angel came to Mary and said, "Peace be with you. The Lord is with you and has greatly blessed you.
Mary was deeply troubled by the angel's message. The angel said to her, "Don't be afraid Mary. God has been gracious to you. You will become pregnant and give birth to a Son and you will name him Jesus.
Mary said to the angel, "How can this be?"
The angel answered, "The Holy Spirit will come upon you and God's power will rest upon you."
"For there is nothing that God cannot do."
"I am the Lord's servant," said Mary, "may it happen to me as you have said."

7 Comment on reading

The second Advent figure is Mary. We think of her life from the Annunciation of the angel telling her that she was to be the mother of the Lord to the arrival at Bethlehem, where Jesus was born. Mary can teach us how to welcome Jesus into our hearts and lives. Mary's vocation was unique to be the Mother of God, which was to bring Jesus, the Son of God, into the world. The vocation of each one of us is also unique: we aim to bring Jesus and his love into our world. Mary's response was instant and generous.

8 Response to reading

The figures of Mary and Joseph are placed in the empty crib.

In the silence of our hearts let us listen to God, and like Mary, say "yes" to something he asks of us. [*silent pause*]

10 Thought-Word-Phrase for the day

Let what you have said be done to me

9 Prayers

Like Mary we too believe in God's promise and pray.

[a] That all who are faced with difficult decisions may be guided by the Holy Spirit.
Response: **My soul proclaims the greatness of the Lord.**

[b] That all parents and carers may be blessed.
Response: **My soul proclaims the greatness of the Lord.**

[c] That all world leaders and governments may be generous and caring for the poor.
Response: **My soul proclaims the greatness of the Lord.**

[d] That our schools, homes and parishes will prepare well for your coming this Christmas.
Response: **My soul proclaims the greatness of the Lord.**

[e] That we will be thoughtful and loving at this time.
Response: **My soul proclaims the greatness of the Lord.**

[f] [other prayers]
Response: **My soul proclaims the greatness of the Lord.**

[g] Our Father (perhaps sung)

11 Blessing

May the Lord bless us as we journey through Advent. May he open our ears to his call, our minds to his will and our hearts to say, "Yes" to his love. Amen

12 Concluding song or music

CFE
686 The Angel Gabriel from heaven came

Just before Christmas

1 Entrance music (tape or CD) Choose of suitable carol

2 Introduction

Christmas is drawing close. There are more and more signs of it on the radio, TV, in shops and on posters. There is a lot of glitter. There is a possibility that the real meaning of Christmas could be missed. Christmas is about remembering that Jesus came into our world, and remains with us. He wants us to continue his message of love and peace. The stable of Bethlehem must become the stable of our hearts.

3 Focus or symbol

- Crib
- Advent wreath
- Poster or overhead: *"The people who walked in darkness have seen a great light."*

4 Sign of the Cross

The Cross is a reminder that God loved the world so much that he sent his only Son to save us. We thank him for such great love. So we begin "In the name of the Father and of the Son and of the Holy Spirit."

5 Hymn or song

CFE

366 Light the Advent candle

648 Sing it in the valleys

6 Reading

Isaiah 9:2

The people who walked in darkness have seen a great light. They lived in a land of shadows, but now light is shining on them.

7 Comment on reading

A constant feature of Christmas decorations is light. We see coloured lights on trees, in shops, on the streets. Many who see Christmas lights will hardly remember that the reason for lights at Christmas is the reading we have just heard. When we say that Jesus is the light of the world, we are thinking also about the darkness. The darkness of the world is sin, anger, hatred, division, violence, greed, and selfishness of every kind. Jesus came to point another way, so that the most characteristic Christian word about Christmas is not "merry" but rather "PEACE."

8 Response to reading

CFE		O&N
643	(verse 1)	477

10 Thought-Word-Phrase for the day

Christmas lights can remind us of Jesus who is the Light of the World

9 Prayers

We pray to Jesus, the Prince of peace.

[a] That all who live in darkness may walk in light.
Response: **Come Prince of Peace.**

[b] We pray for continuing peace and justice in these islands, especially in the North of Ireland and all the troubled areas of our world.
Response: **Come Prince of Peace.**

[c] We pray for harmony and good race relations.
Response: **Come Prince of Peace.**

[d] We pray for all who find Christmas difficult – those with addictions, those who are lonely, those who are poor, those with unhappy family situations.
Response: **Come Prince of Peace.**

[e] We pray for ourselves that we may receive peace in our hearts at Christmas, and that we may share some peace with others.
Response: **Come Prince of Peace.**

[f] [other prayers]
Response: **Come Prince of Peace.**

[g] Our Father (perhaps sung)

11 Blessing

May the blessing of the Father, Son and Spirit come down upon us and on all whom we love. May we receive the true spirit of Christmas love, joy and peace. Amen.

12 Concluding song or music

CFE		O&N
10	(Supp) Christ be our Light	
202	Go tell it on the mountains	187

The Season

1 Entrance music (tape or CD) Choose a suitable piece of music

2 Introduction

Each year the Church has a time of special reflection in Spring. In our homes we often have "Spring-cleaning" when the brighter sun shows up cobwebs and dust that we did not notice in the duller light of winter. Using the light of Christ we are to look at our lives and see what is there that we might sweep out, or clean out. We also look more positively and see what special good thing we might concentrate on.

3 Focus or symbol

- Lenten liturgical drape or poster. The words *"Come back to me"* on overhead or poster.

4 Sign of the Cross

The difficulties of life are often called a cross. These can be carried if we are joined to Jesus and his Cross, and so we say, "In the name of the Father and of the Son and of the Holy Spirit. Amen."

5 Hymn or song

CFE		*O&N*
122	Come back to me with all your heart	683

6 Reading

Joel 2:13

Come back to the Lord your God.
He is kind and full of mercy;
He is patient and keeps his promise.
He is always ready to forgive and not punish.

7 Comment on reading

We hear of people giving up things for Lent, like sweets, or for grown-ups smoking or drinking. It is good to give something up deliberately: it is training, so that when there is something sinful in question, we will have a stronger will-power to say "no" to what is wrong. But the Christian is not just one who learns to say "no." We must also learn to say "yes" to God and to what is good. In the reading from the prophet Joel we heard that God is kind and full of mercy. In Lent we are invited to be kind. There are many people who need cheering up, who need a kind word. There are lonely people who have not many friends; there are lonely pupils that others do not like too much. We can be nice to people at Lent. We can be considerate and avoid hurting people. We can try to be pleasant at home and at school.

8 Response to reading

We have silence for a minute so that we can think of something good that we should aim at during this Lent.

10 Thought-Word-Phrase for the day

What kind act can I do today?

9 Prayers

We pray for the Church and for ourselves this Lent.

[a]	That many people may hear the call of love this Lent.
Response:	**The Lord is kind and patient.**
[b]	That we may be generous to the poor and the lonely.
Response:	**The Lord is kind and patient.**
[c]	That we may be more thoughtful and caring towards all we live, work and play with.
Response:	**The Lord is kind and patient.**
[d]	That people with addictions may be helped and strengthened this Lent.
Response:	**The Lord is kind and patient.**
[e]	That those whose hearts are hard may know comfort and gentleness.
Response:	**The Lord is kind and patient.**
[f]	[other prayers]
Response:	**The Lord is kind and patient.**
[g]	Our Father (perhaps sung)

11 Blessing

May the Lord bless us as we begin our Lenten journey in peace, in forgiveness, in joy and in loving service of others. Amen

12 Concluding song or music

CFE		*O&N*
175	Follow me, follow me	145
567	O Lord, all the world belongs to you	403

Giving things up

1 Entrance music (tape or CD) Choose a suitable piece of music

2 Introduction

Lent is a period of forty days which commemorate the forty days fast of Jesus in the desert and which are a preparation for Easter. It is a time of invitation to come to know Jesus more closely. We look at what we may give up as well as things we can do as we follow in the footsteps of the Master.

3 Focus or symbol

- Outline of footstep/footsteps with phrases such as:
  "Follow me," "Forgive,"
  "Be a peacemaker,"
  "Love as I have loved you,"
  "Renew your life."

4 Sign of the Cross

The deepest meaning of Lent is love, and the Cross is a reminder of Christ's love for us. So we begin "In the name of the Father and of the Son and of the Holy Spirit."

5 Hymn or song

CFE		*O&N*
399	Love is his word	388
567	O Lord, all the world belongs to you	403

6 Reading

Matthew 22:34-39

A teacher of the Law tried to trap Jesus with a question: "Which is the greatest commandment in the Law?" Jesus answered, "Love the Lord your God with all your heart, with all your soul and with all your mind. This is the greatest and most important commandment. The second most important commandment is like it: love your neighbour as you love yourself."

7 Comment on reading

The religious leaders at the time were jealous of Jesus, because the people were crowding around him rather than them. They thought too that he was not religious enough, because he was not telling people to keep the elaborate law that they as religious leaders taught as God's will for all. But Jesus escapes the trap set by his enemies, for he goes to the heart of religion, to the very basis of human society. He shows that the point of giving things up is in order to be more loving.

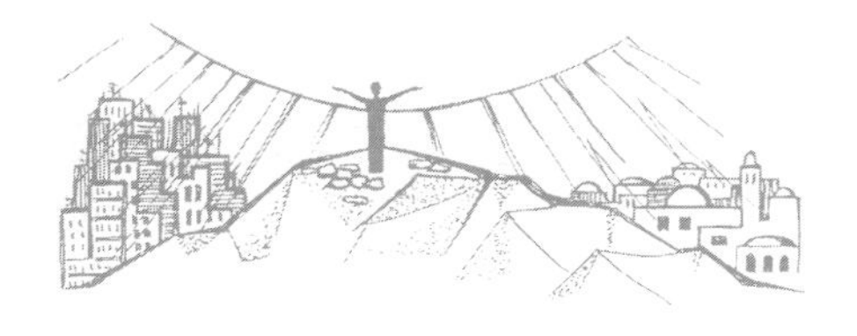

8 Response to reading

Is there some little selfishness in my life that I can give up for Lent, so that I can be more loving? In silence we think of one thing we can give up for Lent.

10 Thought-Word-Phrase for the day

When I am tempted to give in to something wrong this day, I shall say, "Jesus help me."

9 Prayers

We pray that during this Lent we come to know and love Jesus more.

[a]	That all who are in need may receive help.
Response:	**Lord help me to love you more.**
[b]	That those who are better off may be generous to those poorer than themselves.
Response:	**Lord help me to love you more.**
[c]	That all who are angry and bitter may forgive.
Response:	**Lord help me to love you more.**
[d]	That we may continue strong in our decisions or resolutions this Lent.
Response:	**Lord help me to love you more.**
[e]	That our homes, school and parish may be blessed this Lent.
Response:	**Lord help me to love you more.**
[f]	[other prayers]
[g]	Our Father (perhaps sung)

11 Blessing

May the Lord bless us on our Lenten journey. May his love and strength support us all day long. Amen.

12 Concluding song or music

CFE		*O&N*
295	If God is for us	231

Taking things up

1 Entrance music (tape or CD)
Choose a suitable piece of music

2 Introduction

Challenges are good for us. The school is a challenge for all – both teachers and pupils. There are challenges apart from the classroom: games, playtime, football, drama, swimming, outdoor activities, school outings. People often think of Lent as a time for giving things up, but it is perhaps more important to think of it as a time to take things up. Since it is a time for new challenges, it should be a time for taking up something that will help to improve our way of life and be helpful or caring for others.

3 Focus or symbol

(see Lent 2)

- Outline of footstep/footsteps with phrases such as:

  "Follow me," "Forgive,"
  "Be a peacemaker,"
  "Love as I have loved you,"
  "Renew your life."

4 Sign of the Cross

The Cross is a constant reminder that Jesus took up a very costly challenge for love of me, and so in gratitude we begin, "In the name of the Father and of the Son and of the Holy Spirit."

5 Hymn or song

CFE		*O&N*
572	Oh the word of my Lord	431

6 Reading

John 15:14

Jesus said, "You are my friends, if you do what I command you."

7 Comment on reading

It is great to hear that Jesus regards us as his friends. But other people are his friends too, and he wants his friends to be our friends also. Friendship with Jesus also means that we do as he did, going out in warmth and loving tenderness to all, the weak, the homeless, the unloved, the sick, the poor. Can I make someone just a teeny bit happier today?

8 Response to reading

In the silence of your heart think of someone that you find it really hard to love and then pray for that person now.

10 Thought-Word-Phrase for the day

What small kind act could I do for someone whom I find it really hard to love?

9 Prayers

We pray with confidence to our loving Father:

[a] That we may go out with warm hearts to all.
Response: **Warm our hearts with your love.**

[b] That we may always see the good in others.
Response: **Warm our hearts with your love.**

[c] That we may bring peace and forgiveness to our homes, school and parish.
Response: **Warm our hearts with your love.**

[d] That we may be more generous with our time and our pocket money.
Response: **Warm our hearts with your love.**

[e] That the people we find really hard to love may be blessed in every way.
Response: **Warm our hearts with your love.**

[f] [other prayers]
Response: **Warm our hearts with your love.**

[g] Our Father (perhaps sung)

11 Blessing

May the Lord bless us this day.
May he open our eyes and enlarge our hearts to see him and meet him in others today. Amen.

12 Concluding song or music

CFE		*O&N*
799	Whatsoever you do	606
	Our God sent his Son long ago *with its response:* Become the Good News you have heard	435

Going apart to the mountain of God

1 Entrance music (tape or CD)
Choose a suitable piece of music

2 Introduction

There are times when we all want to be alone or to be left alone to gather ourselves together or think things out. Some of the favourite places for people to be alone are outdoors, on a common, in a field, in the countryside, or seaside, and especially on hills or mountains. Jesus liked to escape and be alone on a mountain to talk to his Father. Sometimes he took his disciples along so that they could be alone with him. Assembly time is a space in the day when we drop other things to be alone with God, even though we are with others. He will teach us and love us and draw us to his Son Jesus.

3 Focus or symbol

– Picture, poster or sketch of a mountain.

4 Sign of the Cross

At baptism we are signed with the Cross and set apart as sons and daughters of the Father and as brothers and sisters of Jesus Christ. And so we begin "In the name of the Father and of the Son and of the Holy Spirit."

5 Hymn or song

CFE		*O&N*
283	I saw the grass	
369	Like a shepherd, he feeds his flock	727

6 Reading

Matthew 17:2-8 (paraphrased)

Jesus took Peter, James and John and led them up Mount Tabor, a high mountain, where they were alone. As they looked on, a change came over Jesus; his clothes became shining white. Peter spoke up and said: "Teacher, it is good for us to be here." Then a cloud appeared and God's voice came from the cloud, "This is my own dear Son, listen to him." They took a quick look around but they did not see anybody else there; only Jesus was with them.

7 Comment on reading

We may not be able to find a mountain on which to pray, but we can always find Jesus when we give some moments to draw our lives together, to see how things are going, to ask for God's help. These quiet moments are precious, and we need some each day. But we have to have our eyes open to other times in which God may speak to us: he may speak through a nice view, through a bird's song, through the beauty of the stars or moon, through somebody needing a helping hand.

8 Response to reading

We too are sons and daughters of God. In silence let us hear God's personal word to each of us: "you are my son; you are my daughter."

10 Thought-Word-Phrase for the day

Seek the Lord at all times

9 Prayers

On the mountain Peter, James and John experienced the presence of God. As God's sons and daughters we confidently pray:

[a] That people may hear your voice and welcome your word to them today.
Response: **Lord it is good to be here.**

[b] That those who are trapped in fear or in addictions may be set free.
Response: **Lord it is good to be here.**

[c] That our Church may be alive with the wonder of your presence.
Response: **Lord it is good to be here.**

[d] That we may recognise and respect your presence in the Bible, in the Eucharist, in the wonders of nature and in each other.
Response: **Lord it is good to be here.**

[e] That we may learn to set aside quiet moments to listen to your voice.
Response: **Lord it is good to be here.**

[f] [other prayers]
Response: **Lord it is good to be here.**

[g] Our Father (perhaps sung)

11 Blessing

May the Lord bless us.
May he cast all fears from our hearts.
May he warm us with his loving presence as we journey through the day. Amen.

12 Concluding song or music

CFE		*O&N*
799	Whatsoever you do	606
	We behold the splendour of God	587

The Poor

1 Entrance music (tape or CD) Choose a suitable piece of music

2 Introduction

One of the best-known sayings of Jesus is "You will always have the poor with you" (John 12:8). One of the great themes for Lent is care of the poor, which in the past was seen as giving some money to those who are worse off than ourselves. But who are the poor? Who would we class as "worse off than ourselves?" It is not only those who are hungry as in countries abroad. There are those indeed who do not have enough money, who are undernourished, and hungry. But there are people who are in deep need in other ways too. Loneliness, depression, drug-addiction, unhappy homes are places of poverty, even if there are nice carpets and two cars at the gate. In Lent we think about all the people who are poor in whatever way. This will be the obviously poor, like the homeless. We can ask what we might do to help even in a little way those who are poor in this sense. But what about the others? We can pray for them to-day and during Lent; perhaps we can have a chance to do some kindness to somebody who is unhappy and poor, even if their neighbours think they are well off.

3 Focus or symbol

- CAFOD posters and display materials.

4 Sign of the Cross

All of us, those who are rich and those who are poor, can be united in the Sign of the Cross, and so we begin, "In the name of the Father and of the Son and of the Holy Spirit."

5 Hymn or song

CFE		*O&N*
307	In the land there is a hunger	
567	O Lord, all the world belongs to you	403

6 Reading *Luke 4:16-20*

In the synagogue at his home town of Nazareth, Jesus was given the book of Isaiah from which he read:

> The spirit of the Lord is upon me,
> Because he has chosen me
> To bring good news to the poor.
> He has sent me to proclaim liberty
> to the captives
> And recovery of sight to the blind;
> To set free the oppressed,
> and announce that the time has come
> when the Lord will save his people.

Then Jesus said that with him this great promise was coming true in him.

7 Comment on reading

The *Catechism of the Catholic Church* tells us that God blesses all who help the poor, and part of the constant tradition of the Church is it's love for the poor. It says too: "When we attend the needs of those in want, we give them what is really theirs." There are many works of mercy. These can be looking after spiritual or bodily needs. Spiritual works of mercy include instructing, advising, consoling, comforting, forgiving, bearing wrongs patiently. Corporal works of mercy include feeding the hungry, sheltering the homeless, clothing the naked, visiting the sick and imprisoned and burying the dead. The Peruvian saint, St. Rose of Lima said, "When we serve the poor and the sick, we serve Jesus. We must not fail to help our neighbours, because in them we serve Jesus." (arts. 2443-2449).

8 Response to Reading

Something that the school could do for those in need, e.g. remind them or the school's chosen charities, or deciding on some small project.

10 Thought-Word-Phrase for the day

Can I give even a little money today for the poor and do some kindly act?

9 Prayers

We hold before God the needy of the world.

[a] We pray for all who have spiritual needs, those without hope, those depressed, those grieving, those far from God.
Response: **Lord, give us generous hearts.**

[b] We pray for the victims of famine, disasters, war, those exploited or oppressed, the victims of dictatorships and cruel governments.
Response: **Lord, give us generous hearts.**

[c] We pray for all who are homeless, for refugees, for all who are treated as outcasts and for all who feel they cannot cope.
Response: **Lord, give us generous hearts.**

[d] We pray for those who work to serve the poor abroad, for relief agencies, for the Red Cross, for Amnesty International and for CAFOD [*other agencies may also be mentioned*]
Response: **Lord, give us generous hearts.**

[e] We pray for all who care for those in need in our own area, for good neighbours, for St. Vincent de Paul and voluntary and statutory bodies.
Response: **Lord, give us generous hearts.**

[f] [other prayers]
Response: **Lord, give us generous hearts.**

[g] Our Father (perhaps sung)

11 Blessing

The grace of our Lord Jesus Christ, the love of God and the fellowship of the Holy Spirit be with us all. Amen.

12 Concluding song or music

CFE		*O&N*
376	Look around you, can you see?	316
385	Lord make me an instrument of thy peace	328
478	Make me a channel of thy peace	342

The Bethany Visit

1 Entrance music (tape or CD) Choose a suitable piece of music

2 Introduction

A visit from a special friend can be very enriching. We enjoy the time together, and afterwards we get pleasure thinking about the visit. Jesus visits us in many ways. One of the lovely stories of his visits was to the house of Simon, a man he had healed. This mealtime was a chance for his friends to do something for Jesus.

3 Focus or symbol

- Some icon of Jesus with a scented candle or perfumed oil

4 Sign of the Cross

At baptism with water, the word of God and the holy oil were sealed forever as belonging to the Trinity, and so we begin "In the name of the Father and of the Son and of the Holy Spirit."

5 Hymn or song

CFE		O&N
128	Come, Lord Jesus, come	104
347	Lay your hand gently on us	295

6 Reading

Mark 14:3-9 [paraphrased]

Jesus visited Simon, a man whom he had cured of leprosy. During the meal a women came in with a jar of very expensive lotion worth hundreds of pounds. She broke open the jar and poured the contents on Jesus. Some of the people present were very angry with this woman, as they thought she was wasting the oil. Indeed she could have sold it to help the poor, they said. But Jesus answered them that this was a special day because he was visiting them; they could show kindness to the poor at other times. He not only defended the woman, but also praised her kindness to him before his approaching death.

7 Comment on reading

Here we have several visits. Jesus visits the man he had healed. The man may be showing his thanks by inviting Jesus; Jesus may be following up the healing with a visit to complete the man's full recovery. But then there is a surprise visitor who comes to show special love for Jesus, a woman with a big generous heart. Jesus was very touched by her kindness.

8 Response to reading

Is there someone we could give pleasure to by a visit: a neighbour, a sick or elderly person might be heartened by a little kindness from us?

10 Thought-Word-Phrase for the day

God visits us in many ways

9 Prayers

God's visit to his people in Jesus Christ invites us in turn to ask a blessing on all who visit.

[a] We pray that the Church may always welcome the coming of Jesus.
Response: **Come to visit us, Lord.**

[b] We pray that we be welcoming to all visitors to our school.
Response: **Come to visit us, Lord.**

[c] We pray for those who visit others in need: public health nurses, social workers, members of St. Vincent de Paul, voluntary workers, and chaplains.
Response: **Come to visit us, Lord.**

[d] We pray for those who are in need of a visit, the housebound, the lonely, prisoners.
Response: **Come to visit us, Lord.**

[e] We pray for those who come to our country as tourists, that they may have a pleasant and trouble-free visit.
Response: **Come to visit us, Lord.**

[f] [other prayers]
Response: **Come to visit us, Lord.**

[g] Our Father (perhaps sung)

11 Blessing

Numbers 6:24-26

May the Lord bless and take care of you.
May the Lord be kind and gracious to you.
May the Lord look on you with favour
and give you peace. Amen.

12 Concluding song or music

CFE		O&N
203	Go the Mass is ended	188
	Come and go with me	89

The King comes to Jerusalem

1 Entrance music (tape or CD) Choose a suitable piece of music

2 Introduction

Jesus rode into Jerusalem on a donkey and the cheering crowd welcomed him as the Messiah, the long-awaited One. They laid their cloaks on the ground for him to walk on, as a sign of respect; they waved palm branches. It was a welcome such as kings received at that time.

3 Focus or symbol

- The bible and palm branches
- an overhead could be used with words such as Hosanna, King, Messiah.

4 Sign of the Cross

Jesus is not king in our sense; the Cross on which he was executed carried the words: "Jesus of Nazareth, King of the Jews." And so we begin "In the name of the Father and of the Son and of the Holy Spirit."

5 Hymn or song

CFE		*O&N*
265	Hosanna, loud Hosanna	
268	How lovely on the mountains (vv. 1–4)	223

6 Reading

Mark 11:1-11 (paraphrased)

As Jesus and his disciples approached Jerusalem they came to the Mount of Olives. Jesus sent two of his disciples on ahead to a village with the instruction that they should bring a donkey that was tied up and waiting for them. They brought the donkey to Jesus and spread their cloaks over it and on the road. People cheered and chanted, "Praise God. Blessed is he who comes in the name of the Lord! Blessings to God for the King of Israel. Hosanna in the highest."

7 Comment on reading

God's ways are not our ways. The Jews in the Old Testament expected a glorious King to come as a political leader. God's way was to send His Son as a humble King who would set them free not by terrorism or by a popular uprising, but by dying on the Cross. The kingdom he left, and of which we are members by baptism, is not a showy one, but a community under Christ the King which will be committed to "truth and life, holiness and grace, justice, love and peace." (See *Vatican II, Church, LG 36*)

8 Response to reading

The bible is carried around the hall with a crucifix and some palm branches and candles. The rest of the assembly sing a hymn such as:

CFE		O&N
190	Give me joy in my heart	159
698	The King of glory comes, the nation rejoices	527

Thought-Word-Phrase for the day

"Your kingdom come."

9 Prayers

With confident hope we pray to Jesus our King that the marks of his Kingdom may appear in our midst:

[a] That the peoples may be committed to the values of truth and life.
Response: **You are the King of glory.**

[b] That the Church may grow in holiness and grace.
Response: **You are the King of glory.**

[c] That all who have responsibility for law in our society may serve the cause of justice.
Response: **You are the King of glory.**

[d] That we may show by our lives that love which is the supreme mark of the Kingdom.
Response: **You are the King of glory.**

[e] That places in conflict (*name some*_____) may find the ways of peace.
Response: **You are the King of glory.**

[f] [other prayers]
Response: **You are the King of glory.**

[g] Our Father (perhaps sung)

11 Blessing

May Jesus our King bless us this day and help us to walk in the ways of truth and life, holiness and grace, justice, love and peace. Amen.

12 Concluding Song or Music

CFE		O&N
801	When I survey the wondrous Cross	610

or play tape of "The Holy City" by Stephen Adams.

The Last Supper

1 Entrance music (tape or CD) Choose a suitable piece of music

2 Introduction

Some days after his entry into Jerusalem riding a donkey and proclaimed as Messiah-King, it was obvious to Jesus that he would soon die. He wanted to die to save us, but he also wanted to remain with us. His solution was, through the Last Supper, to establish the Eucharist or Mass as a way in which he could remain always with his followers as they commemorated his death on Calvary.

3 Focus or symbol

- Poster/print of Last Supper scene,

  and/or
- copy of Bishops' document, 'One Bread One Body',

  and/or
- chalice with some bread and grapes.

4 Sign of the Cross

At every Mass we begin with the sign of the Cross reminding us of our baptism by which we were claimed as Christ's followers through his death on Calvary. And so we begin "In the name of the Father and of the Son and of the Holy Spirit."

5 Hymn or song

CFE		*O&N*
4	A new commandment I give unto you	39
730	This is my body	556

6 Reading

Mark 14:22-26

While they were eating, Jesus took a piece of bread and gave a prayer of thanks, broke it and gave it to his disciples and said, "Take it, this is my body." Then he took a cup, gave thanks to God and handed it to them and they all drank it. Jesus said, "This is my blood which will be poured out for many"...They sang a hymn and went out to the Mount of Olives.

7 Response to reading

The Church teaches us: "At the Last Supper, on the night he was betrayed, our Saviour gave us the Eucharistic sacrifice of his body and blood. This he did in order to carry on the sacrifice of the Cross throughout the ages until he should come again. He has thus given to us in the Church, a memorial of his death and resurrection: a sacrament of love, a sign of unity, a bond of love, a paschal meal in which Christ is received, our minds are filled with grace and we are given the hope of our future glory." (*Vatican II, Liturgy SC 47* – paraphrased)

8 Response to reading

Some children walk around the hall showing the main Mass vestments: alb, stole and chasuble.

10 Thought-Word-Phrase for the day

"O sacrament most holy, O sacrament divine, all praise and all thanksgiving be every moment thine."

9 Prayers

We pray for a deep love of the Mass and that its benefits may be shared by the world.

[a] That all who celebrate the Eucharist – priests and people – may be blessed and holy.
Response: **You are the Bread of Life.**

[b] That all who are preparing for First Communion may remain close to you always.
Response: **You are the Bread of Life.**

[c] That parents, catechists and teachers who prepare others to receive the sacraments may lead also by the example of their lives.
Response: **You are the Bread of Life.**

[d] That those Christians who are separated from us, and others who cannot receive Holy Communion with us, may be drawn into its unity and blessings.
Response: **You are the Bread of Life.**

[e] That all who have died may through the Mass be brought into the fullness of life.
Response: **You are the Bread of Life.**

[f] [other prayers]
Response: **You are the Bread of Life.**

[g] Our Father (perhaps sung)

11 Blessing

The grace of our Lord Jesus Christ, the love of God and the fellowship of the Holy Spirit be with you. Amen.

12 Concluding song or music

CFE		*O&N*
271/272	I am the Bread of Life	225/226
578	One Bread one Body	744

Good Friday

1 Entrance music (tape or CD) Choose a suitable piece of music

2 Introduction

At first sight one might wonder why "Good Friday" is so called. It was a day of violence, of anger, a day of the terrible murder of the innocent Son of God. But it was good for us, because on that day God's love conquered evil and death; on that day we are saved from sin, punishment and endless death.

3 Focus or symbol

- Large wooden Cross with white drape, or a crucifix.

4 Sign of the Cross

The deepest meaning of Calvary is love, and the Cross is a reminder of God's love for us. So we begin "In the name of the Father and of the Son and of the Holy Spirit."

5 Hymn or song

CFE		O&N
40	Amazing Grace	36
187	From heaven you came (The Servant King)	

6 Reading

[Texts from the Passion narratives: Matthew 27; Mark 15; Luke 23; John 19]

At nine o'clock in the morning they crucified him between two bandits. During the next three hours he spoke seven times:

"Father forgive them, they know not what they do."
"My God, my God why have you forsaken me?"
To the thief on his right: "This day you will be with me in paradise.
To Mary and the beloved disciple: "Woman this is your son… this is your mother."
"I thirst."
"Into your hands I commend my spirit."
"It is finished."

7 Comment on reading

These precious last words of Jesus are set before us as a pattern for our lives: we are to forgive, we are to trust in God, we are to accept Mary as our mother, we are to continue to do God's will to the end.

8 Response to reading

The Cross is held up or carried around the hall as the assembly sings Taizé chant, "Jesus remember me" and/or:

CFE		O&N
791	Were you there when they crucified my Lord?	598

10 Thought-Word-Phrase for the day

Christ has died, Christ is risen,
Christ will come again.

9 Prayers

We pray that the world may be healed through the Cross of Christ.

[a] For leaders of our Church that they may be compassionate and forgiving.

Response: **Lord by your Cross and resurrection you have set us free.**

[b] For continuing peace in the North of Ireland which began with the Good Friday Agreement.

Response: **Lord by your Cross and resurrection you have set us free.**

[c] For all who suffer from injustice that they may be set free.

Response: **Lord by your Cross and resurrection you have set us free.**

[d] For all the sick and the dying that they may be clothed with Christ's healing love

Response: **Lord by your Cross and resurrection you have set us free.**

[e] For all Christians that they may never be ashamed of the Cross of our Lord Jesus Christ.

Response: **Lord by your Cross and resurrection you have set us free.**

[f] [other prayers]

Response: **Lord by your Cross and resurrection you have set us free.**

[g] Our Father (perhaps sung)

11 Blessing

May the Cross of Jesus be our light, our hope and our consolation. Amen.

12 Concluding song or music

CFE		O&N
383	Lord Jesus Christ, you have come to us	326

The Resurrection

1 Entrance music (tape or CD)

Choose a suitable piece of music that uses the word *alleluia*.

2 Introduction

We gather to think about and to give thanks for the central mystery of the Christian faith, that Jesus rose from the dead and lives among us through his Holy Spirit.

3 Focus or symbol

- White drape and Cross
  or
  poster of Resurrection.
- With banner/overhead and the words *"Alleluia" or Jesus is risen, Alleluia"*

4 Sign of the Cross

Good Friday and Easter cannot be separated, and so as we celebrate Easter, we begin with the Sign of the Cross, "In the name of the Father and of the Son and of the Holy Spirit."

5 Hymn or song

CFE		*O&N*
38	Alleluia, this is the day	
326	Jesus is Lord	280
	Hallelujah, my Father	199

6 Reading

Luke 24: 1-12 (paraphrased)

Very early on Easter morning the women went to the tomb with scented oils to embalm the body of Jesus. They found that the big stone that had been at the entry to the tomb was rolled away. But when they peered into the cave, the body of Jesus was not there. They were puzzled and upset about this. They wanted to do the best they could for the dead body of Jesus. Then suddenly, two angels appeared in bright shining clothes, who said to them, "why are you looking here for one who is alive. He is not here; he has been raised." The angels then reminded them of God's great plan which was that Jesus was to suffer, be crucified, and then rise in glory.

7 Comment on reading

This story about the empty tomb was hard for the early Church to believe. At first the apostles did not believe the women's story. But then later, when Jesus appeared to them, they believed. We can easily be disheartened by disappointment, just as the disciples were. But they heard the good news about the Resurrection and began to believe. Jesus is still with us, at mass, and through his Holy Spirit. We have to learn to believe that whatever darkness we may experience, Jesus is there with us to strengthen us and give us hope.

8 Response to reading

CFE		O&N
731	This is the day	560

10 Thought-Word-Phrase for the day

Christ is risen

9 Prayers

We give thanks to the Risen Lord as we pray.

[a] For the gift of life with all its wonder and beauty.
Response: **We thank you, alleluia.**

[b] For our baptism and our new life in you.
Response: **We thank you, alleluia.**

[c] For the marvel of your presence in the Eucharist.
Response: **We thank you, alleluia.**

[d] For coming to us in the Bible and in our lives.
Response: **We thank you, alleluia.**

[e] For all who work to protect and safeguard life.
Response: **We thank you, alleluia.**

[f] [other prayers]
Response: **We thank you, alleluia.**

[g] Our Father (perhaps sung)

11 Blessing

May the living Lord bless us.
May he heal us of all selfishness.
May he lead us to be holy and caring. Amen.

12 Concluding song or music

CFE		O&N
32	Alleluia, alleluia, give thanks to the Risen Lord	14
728	Thine be the Glory	554

Easter 2

Life

1 Entrance music (tape or CD) Choose a suitable piece of music that uses the word *alleluia.*

2 Introduction

Life and death are the two most important events for everybody. Jesus, who died on the Cross for us, rose up again alive on Easter Day. We reflect today on life and pray with thanksgiving.

3 Focus or symbol

- Plant or goldfish
- Poster depicting life such as a baby, nature, animal, plants.
- Overhead with words, *"I am the way, the Truth and the Life"* (see John 14:6)

4 Sign of the Cross

It is through the Cross of Jesus that we come into new life, and so we begin "In the name of the Father and of the Son and of the Holy Spirit."

5 Hymn or song

CFE		*O&N*
513	Now the green blade riseth	376
543	Centre of my life	
	New daytime is dawning	370

6 Reading

Romans 6:4

By our baptism, then, we are buried with him and share his death, in order that, just as Christ was raised from the dead, by the glorious power of the Father, so we too might live a new life.

7 Comment on reading

Life is all around us, in gardens, on patches of ground, in the sky. When something is alive, we see that it moves or grows. We began to move and grow as Christians with baptism. We are brought into new life. Our life grows when we try to follow the way of Jesus Christ, who wants to lead us to himself, since he is the Way, the Life and the Truth. We are called to support life, to avoid being cruel to others, to oppose bullying, to be kind to animals, to respect plants and flowers.

8 Response to reading

The wonder of life... What can I do to promote life?

10 Thought-Word-Phrase for the day

Open our eyes to see the wonder of life around us

9 Prayers

We give thanks for the gift of life.

[a]	That we may never take the gift of live for granted.
Response:	**We thank you for the gift of life.**
[b]	That those whose life is threatened may be saved.
Response:	**We thank you for the gift of life.**
[c]	That people would take more care for life on our roads.
Response:	**We thank you for the gift of life.**
[d]	That those who care for life, especially doctors and nurses, parents and social workers may be generous and loving.
Response:	**We thank you for the gift of life.**
[e]	That we may respect all life, especially those who are helpless and weak, and also all birds, animals and plants.
Response:	**We thank you for the gift of life.**
[f]	[other prayers]
Response:	**We thank you for the gift of life.**
[g]	Our Father (perhaps sung)

11 Blessing

May the Risen Lord of Life bless us this day with all good gifts and fill our hearts and minds with new life.

12 Concluding song or music

CFE		*O&N*
95	Bread of Life	
275	Lord of the Dance	
	New life! New life!	371

The Risen Lord

1 Entrance music (tape or CD)

Choose a suitable piece of music that uses the word *alleluia.*

2 Introduction

Christ overcame not only death, but also sin. He wants to share his victory with us and bring us into the life of the Trinity, Father, Son and Spirit.

3 Focus or symbol

- Seed, acorn, cone of fir tree, egg, or other symbol of new life.
- Cross with overhead, *"He is risen."*

4 Sign of the Cross

The sign of the Cross reminds us of our life in the Holy Trinity, which came about through the Cross and Resurrection of Jesus. So we begin "In the name of the Father and of the Son and of the Holy Spirit."

5 Hymn or song

CFE		*O&N*
246	He is Lord	206
648	Sing it in the valleys	
	Jesus, you are Lord	286
	or other resurrection hymn	

6 Reading

Acts 2:36-39 (paraphrased)

On Pentecost Day, St. Peter told the Jewish leaders that they had put the Messiah to death on the Cross. But he then declared, "You are to know for sure that Jesus, who was crucified, was made Lord and Messiah." The people were really afraid, but Peter told them that they could have new life if they turned way from sin, believed in Jesus and be baptised.

7 Comment on reading

The traditional symbols of Easter are about life. Eggs remind us of the new life that is a chicken. Lambs are very much alive. Seeds are a promise of life. But there are other resurrection symbols. A person who gets better after serious illness, a drug addict who recovers, a bully who becomes a kind person, are all symbols of new life, resurrection. The big recovery is from sin and darkness, and this we find through baptism so that we are to walk in life and light.

8 Response to reading

Indicate some symbol of new life particular to the school or the area, or hold up a plant. Give thanks for life.

10 Thought-Word-Phrase for the day

The act of faith of St. Thomas: "My Lord and my God"
(John 20:28)

9 Prayers

We turn to our Risen Lord and pray.

[a] Risen Lord, speak to our hearts as you spoke to Mary Magdalene in the quiet of the garden.
Response: **Alleluia.**

[b] Risen Lord walk closely with all who are sad at this time as you walked the Emmaus road with the two disciples.
Response: **Alleluia.**

[c] Risen Lord, may all people receive the Good News about the gospel and come to believe.
Response: **Alleluia.**

[d] Risen Lord, may all who are war hear your words, "Peace be with you."
Response: **Alleluia.**

[e] Risen Lord, may those who find faith difficult be helped by the example of Thomas who learned to leave doubt aside and believe.
Response: **Alleluia.**

[f] [other prayers]
Response: **Alleluia.**

[g] Our Father (perhaps sung)

11 Blessing

May the Risen Lord bless us this day.
May he fill us with the wonder of his loving presence.
May we help to bring love, joy and peace to others. Amen.

12 Concluding song or music

CFE		*O&N*
647	Sing alleluia	479
648	Sing it in the valleys	

Joy

1 Entrance music (tape or CD)

Choose a suitable piece of music that uses the word *alleluia.*

2 Introduction

Joy is one of the deepest desires of people. We say that we en-joyed a game, a party, a TV programme. But so often people seek joy in what is not helpful, or what is destructive like drugs or violence or vandalism. Today we look at joy in another way; we look at Jesus Risen from the dead as a source of joy.

3 Focus or symbol

- Symbol of enjoyment: flowers, CD disc, video, local or school football jersey, poster of beautiful scene, painting.
- Overhead with words, *"Rejoice in the Lord, always"* (Ph 4:4).

4 Sign of the Cross

The source of our Christian joy is in fact the Cross of Jesus, which brought hope and joy to the world. So we begin "In the name of the Father and of the Son and of the Holy Spirit."

5 Hymn or song

CFE		O&N
595	Peace, perfect peace (v.1, 2 and 5)	597
	Fill our hearts with joy and gladness	79

6 Reading

Various scripture texts

"My joy is in the Lord" (Ps 104:34)

The angel said, "Be joyful Mary, the Lord is with you" (Luke 1:28)

The fruit of the Holy Spirit is "love, joy, peace" (Gal 5:22)

"The one who loves wisdom brings joy" (Prov 29:3)

"There is great joy in heaven over one sheep that is found" (Luke 15:6)

"Jesus was full of joy in the Holy Spirit" (Luke 10:21)

"The disciples were full of joy when they saw the Risen Jesus." (Matt 28: 18)

7 Comment on reading

Very often joy only emerges after difficulty or effort. A team that does not train will never win matches; pupils who do not study will not have the joy of passing exams. But even what brings us joy can become boring in time. A favourite track can be played ten times, fifty times. But eventually we do not play it so often. Again, there can be a nice tree on the road, or in the schoolyard or on the way home. We get so used to it that it ceases to bring us pleasure. Most people would love to win the lottery. But we hear so often that this did not bring people lasting happiness. We might be different, or would we? The Christian message is that true joy, joy which lasts can only be found in God, in the ways of Jesus Christ. We may find doing what is right difficult, we may find it painful to be good, but in the end we will not regret it. God's way leads us to a deeper joy than anything we can arrange or search for ourselves.

8 Response to reading

In silence we thank God for people who have brought joy into our lives (*silent pause*).

10 Thought-Word-Phrase for the day

"Be a carrier of God's joy wherever you go."

(*Mother Teresa*)

9 Prayers

We give thanks for the gift of joy.

[a] For all who bring joy to the lives of others in art, music, writing and sport.
Response: **The joy of the Lord is your strength** (*Nehemiah 8:10*).

[b] For the many organisations who bring some joy into the lives of those who are poor or on the margins of our society.
Response: **The joy of the Lord is your strength.**

[c] For greater Christian joy in our homes, schools and parishes.
Response: **The joy of the Lord is your strength.**

[d] For those who go astray in seeking false joys.
Response: **The joy of the Lord is your strength.**

[e] For those who are sad, lonely, depressed, bitter or disappointed.
Response: **The joy of the Lord is your strength.**

[f] [other prayers]
Response: **The joy of the Lord is your strength.**

[g] Our Father (perhaps sung)

11 Blessing

"May the God of hope fill you with all joy"
Amen.

(*Romans 15:13*)

12 Concluding song or music

CFE		*O&N*
190	Give me joy in my heart	159
617	Rejoice in the Lord always	462
	My soul is filled with joy	365

Ascension

1 Entrance music (tape or CD)
Choose a suitable piece of music

2 Introduction

The Ascension celebrates Jesus' final departure into heaven, he ascended. But it is also a celebration of the mission which he left to his Church. The final words of a person before they go away are always recalled. We recall Jesus final words to his Church, which are words of sending.

3 Focus or symbol

- The Mission Statement of the School
- Globe or map of the world

4 Sign of the Cross

We are baptised in the name of the Trinity and so we begin "In the name of the Father and of the Son and of the Holy Spirit."

5 Hymn or song

CFE		*O&N*
477	Majesty, worship his majesty	735

6 Reading

Matt 28:16-20

The eleven disciples went to the hill in Galilee where Jesus had told them to go. When they saw him, they worshipped him, even though some of them doubted. Jesus drew near them and said to them, "I have been given all authority in heaven and on earth. Go, then, to all peoples everywhere and make them my disciples: baptise them in the name of the Father, the Son and the Holy Spirit, and teach them to obey everything I have commanded you. And I am with you always, to the end of the age."

7 Comment on reading

The story of the Ascension is a beautiful mystery, which has many deep messages for the apostles and for us. At various times just before his death and after the Resurrection Jesus tells us what his parting means for us.

"I am with you always" (Matt 28:20)

"I go and prepare a place for you" (John 14:3)

"When the Spirit comes he will lead you into all the truth" (John 16:12)

"I will come back and take you to myself" (John 14:3)

"Go throughout the whole world and preach the Gospel to all" (Mark 16:15)

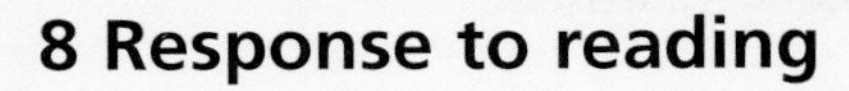

8 Response to reading

Point to map or globe where the Gospel has been preached/indicate where some local person is a missionary.

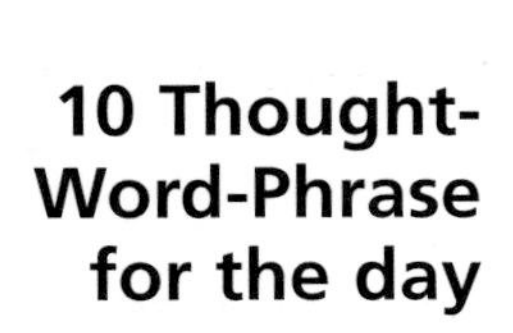

10 Thought-Word-Phrase for the day

Jesus is always with us:
talk to him to-day

9 Prayers

We give thanks for the gift of faith.

[a]	We pray for all who work to spread the Gospel.
Response:	**Christ be beside us.**
[b]	We pray for continuing peace and justice in these islands, especially in the North of Ireland.
Response:	**Christ be beside us.**
[c]	We pray for harmony and good race relations.
Response:	**Christ be beside us.**
[d]	We pray for refugees and exiles.
Response:	**Christ be beside us.**
[e]	We pray for all unjustly imprisoned.
Response:	**Christ be beside us.**
[f]	[other prayers]
Response:	**Christ be beside us.**
[g]	Our Father (perhaps sung)

11 Blessing

May the Lord bless us.
May his promise to be with us warm our hearts.
May we take his message to all that we meet.
Amen.

12 Concluding song or music

CFE		*O&N*
69	Be still and know I am with you	57
201	Go out to the whole world (*round*)	
289	I will be with you	263

The Holy Spirit

1 Entrance music (tape or CD) Choose a suitable piece of music

2 Introduction

The Holy Spirit is called our Helper and our Guide. He helps us and guides us with gifts and further guides us to produce fruits.
In our assemblies during the coming days we will look at some of his gifts such as: Wisdom and understanding and we will give thanks for the fruits of the Spirit in our lives, e.g. love and peace

3 Focus or symbol

- McCrimmon poster - Holy Spirit and Gifts
- Candle
- Overhead with words, *"Come Holy Spirit."*

4 Sign of the Cross

The Cross is a reminder that we have received the Holy Spirit at Baptism, and so we begin, "In the name of the Father, and of the Son and of the Holy Spirit."

5 Hymn or song

CFE		*O&N*
8	Abba Father (three stanzas: 1, 4, 9)	3
118	Colours of day	87

6 Reading *Isaiah 11:2 (paraphrased)*

God promised the Holy Spirit would come on Christ: wisdom, understanding, right judgement, knowledge, strength and reverence.

7 Comment on reading

Jesus sends the Holy Spirit to us with these gifts. The "fruits" of these gifts in our lives are described by St. Paul But the Spirit produces love, joy, peace, patience, kindness, goodness and self-control (Gal. 5: 22-23, 25). The names for the Spirit in the Confirmation ceremony are "Helper" and "Guide." At each moment of our lives we can call upon our Friend, the Holy Spirit that Jesus has sent to us from the Father. The Spirit has given us life, he also gives us the possibility of controlling our lives.

8 Response to reading

We thank the Holy Spirit who has given us his gifts and we can say "sorry" for the times we have not used these gifts and blocked their action in our lives.

10 Thought-Word-Phrase for the day

How can I call on my Helper and Guide today?

9 Prayers

[a] We thank you Jesus that through your Spirit you make us wise, understanding and judging well.
Response: **Come Holy Spirit.**

[b] We thank you Jesus, that through your Spirit you make us strong, knowing and reverent.
Response: **Come Holy Spirit.**

[c] We are sorry Jesus that we often forget these gifts when we are in trouble.
Response: **Come Holy Spirit.**

[d] We thank you Jesus that your Holy Spirit produces nice fruits in our lives.
Response: **Come Holy Spirit.**

[e] We thank you Jesus that in all of us and in those around us there is love, joy and peace.
Response: **Come Holy Spirit.**

[f] We thank you Jesus that people are patient, kind and good to us.
Response: **Come Holy Spirit.**

[g] Help us as we grow in your love to be patient, kind and good to others. May we always be truthful about ourselves and self-controlled.
Response: **Come Holy Spirit.**

[h] [other prayers]
Response: **Come Holy Spirit.**

[i] Our Father [perhaps sung]

11 Blessing

The grace of our Lord Jesus Christ, the love of God and the fellowship of the Holy Spirit be with us all. Amen.

12 Concluding song or music

CFE		*O&N*
227	God's spirit is in my heart	183
268	Holy Spirit of fire	217
388	Shine Jesus shine	
	Come Holy Spirit	98

Wisdom

1 Entrance music (tape or CD)

Choose a suitable piece of music

2 Introduction

We often say about a child or a grown up that they are clever or that they are educated. We do not often say that somebody is wise. To call a person wise is a big compliment. The source of genuine wisdom is the Holy Spirit because wisdom in its full meaning is to see things from God's point of view.

3 Focus or symbol

- Poster with image of dove.
- Overhead with words *"Spirit of Wisdom"*

4 Sign of the Cross

We meet the love of the Holy Spirit for the first time at baptism. The Cross reminds us of that entry into life, and so we begin, "In the name of the Father and of the Son and of the Holy Spirit."

5 Hymn or song

CFE		O&N
664	Spirit of God	
666	Spirit of the living God	501
	Come Holy Spirit	100

6 Reading

1 Kings 3: 4-12 (paraphrased)

In the Old Testament the wisest of all people was King Solomon. When he was a young king, God appeared to him in a dream and asked him what he would like. God was very pleased when Solomon did not ask to be rich, or to win wars, or to live a long life but to be wise in ruling God's people. God gave him so much wisdom that people used to come from all over the world to consult him [see Chapters 9 and 10]

7 Comment on reading

If the Church is to be good, and if our country is to be peaceful and prosperous, leaders must learn to see and do things in God's way. We learn many things in school, like reading, writing and history. We must learn wisdom too. But it cannot be taught like a school lesson. It is only the Holy Spirit that can teach us true wisdom, which we find in an attitude, in a way of looking at things which is God's.

8 Response to reading

In silence we ask God to give us his wisdom so that in our work and play we may always see things in the right way and know what we are to do that is decent, truthful and according to the teaching of Jesus Christ. So that we can follow his way.

10 Thought-Word-Phrase for the day

Teach us wisdom O Lord

9 Prayers

We pray for all who need wisdom.

[a] We pray for priests, for our Bishop and for our Holy Father Pope John Paul II that they will teach us and guide us in God's way.
Response: **Lord teach us your way**

{*In Britain…*
[b] We pray for the Royal Family that they will help our nation to be good.
Response: **Lord teach us your way.**}

[c] We pray for our Government and the opposition parties and for all at the seat of government in ____________ (*name place*) and all in the Civil Service that they will know how to pass good laws and make good decisions affecting peoples' lives.
Response: **Lord teach us your way**

[d] For our leaders, in national and local government that they will always have a special care for the poor and those in need.
Response: **Lord teach us your way**

[e] For our teachers, that they will be wise in helping us to learn and grow up well.
Response: **Lord teach us your way**

[f] For all who love and care for us at home that they will be wise in the things they do and say.
Response: **Lord teach us your way**

[g] For ourselves that we will always speak and act as Jesus would have us do and say.
Response: **Lord teach us your way**

[h] [other prayers]
Response: **Lord teach us your way**

[i] Our Father [perhaps sung]

11 Blessing

The grace of our Lord Jesus Christ, the love of God and the fellowship of the Holy Spirit be with us all. Amen.

12 Concluding song or music

CFE		*O&N*
227	God's Spirit is in my heart	183
714	The Spirit is moving All over the world	26

Reverence

1 Entrance music (tape or CD) Choose a suitable piece of music

2 Introduction

It is hard to be good. Sometimes we do not want to, sometimes we do not know how to. There is too a big problem about how to treat people. The Holy Spirit gives us the gift of reverence so that we treat God, other people, ourselves and the environment the right way.

3 Focus or symbol

– Candle with words:
  Reverence
  For God
  For others
  For myself
  For environment.

4 Sign of the Cross

The Holy Spirit leads us into the mystery of our baptism, which is the foundation for the gift of Christian reverence. And so we begin, "In the name of the Father and of the Son and of the Holy Spirit."

5 Hymn or song

CFE		*O&N*
633	Seek ye first the Kingdom of God	473

6 Reading

Hebrews 5:7 (paraphrased)

In His life on earth Jesus prayed to His Father especially when He was afraid to die on the Cross. Because He was reverent God heard Him.

7 Comment on reading

Jesus treated with respect sinners and all His enemies. He said to the sinful woman that the Jews wanted to execute "I do not condemn you, go in peace but do not sin anymore." Jesus wants us to respect God his Father, who loves us so much, and gives us the Holy Spirit. We must also respect ourselves: it is not good to be negative or angry with ourselves very frequently. We have to respect our bodies, our gifts, our values, and our total selves. We must also respect other people. Finally we need to respect the environment: we may use plants, animals, but must never abuse them. (See *Catechism of the Catholic Church* 2415-2418) But reverence in the end has to be taught by the Holy Spirit who will lead us to have the right attitude and respect for God, for ourselves, for others and for our world.

8 Response to reading

Since everyone is important to God, he wants each of us to treat other people with respect and reverence according to their situations. Let us silently think of people we should show more respect to – perhaps firstly, our own selves.

10 Thought-word-phrase for the day

To respect others today

9 Prayers

We pray for the gift of reverence.

[a] Help us Jesus to have the right approach to those at home, the correct way with grown ups and the proper way with those of our own age.

Response: **Lord give us your gift of reverence**

[b] Help us Jesus to respect you in Church, to respect you in the way we say our prayers and in the way we keep your law of love.

Response: **Lord give us your gift of reverence**

[c] Guide those in authority to show respect to people who are poor, those in difficulties and all who have health and other problems.

Response: **Lord give us your gift of reverence**

[d] Help us respect other people's property, their good name and their bodies.

Response: **Lord give us your gift of reverence**

[e] May we always reverence and respect our own bodies and care for ourselves by doing healthy things.

Response: **Lord give us your gift of reverence**

[f] Help us to care for our world, our environment and keep places beautiful, clean and nice.

Response: **Lord give us your gift of reverence**

[g] Help us in our work and play never to take a mean advantage of others.

Response: **Lord give us your gift of reverence**

[h] Help us to respect all who are different from us in ethnic background, in colour, in religion, and especially those who have special problems.

Response: **Lord give us your gift of reverence**

[i] Our Father [perhaps sung]

11 Blessing

The grace of our Lord Jesus Christ, the love of God and the fellowship of the Holy Spirit be with us all. Amen.

12 Concluding song or music

CFE		*O&N*
388	Shine Jesus Shine	
666	Spirit of the living God	501

Love

1 Entrance music (tape or CD)
Choose a suitable piece of music

2 Introduction

The Holy Spirit is often called the Spirit of love. We think too of the short but strong words of the First letter of John, "God is love" (1 John 4: 8,16). Charity or love, in its twofold reality as love of God and love of others is the summing up of the moral life of the believer. It has God for its source – he makes it possible, and God for its aim – through love we reach God.

3 Focus or symbol

- Name or image of some saint or person noted for charity, or name/poster of school's chosen charity.

4 Sign of the Cross

Through baptism we are brought into the family of God, that is the love of the Trinity, and so we begin, "In the name of the Father and of the Son and of the Holy Spirit. Amen."

5 Hymn or song

CFE		*O&N*
399	Love is his word	338
693	The gift of the Holy Spirit	
	or	
	Jesus loves the little children	

from *We are the Church: Music for primary Schools. Volume 1* (BRES tape) side 2, n.16

6 Reading

1 John 3:17; 4:19-20 (paraphrased)

If rich people close their hearts to people in need, how can they say they love God. We must show our love not only by words but in deeds as well... We love because he loved us first. We cannot love the God we do not see, if we do not love the people we can see.

7 Comment on reading

St. Thérèse of the Child Jesus, the Little Flower, was very anxious to serve God, and she was worried that she was not serving as well as she might. She would have liked to do all sorts of great things to show her great love for God; she would have liked to have been a missionary, even a martyr. Then she learned that the greatest thing she could do was to love. She saw that her vocation was "to be love in the heart of the Church." By her being loving within the walls of her convent, others throughout the world would be helped. Our simple acts of love benefit not only the person we see, but many others too that we cannot know.

8 Response to reading

On a school atlas or globe, have some pupils point out places where there is some special need of love.

or

Ask some pupils to complete the sentence: Love is...

10 Thought-Word-Phrase for the day

To love God with all our hearts... and our neighbour as ourselves

9 Prayers

We bring before the Father of love our weakness in loving God and others, and also all those for whom we have a special concern at this time.

[a] The People of ___________ (*name*) are suffering at this time: May they receive help quickly.

Response: **Help us to love you and to love one another.**

[b] There are many who risk their lives to bring relief and support to others: may they be kept safe, and may their work be blessed.

Response: **Help us to love you and to love one another.**

[c] All people are in need of love: May they meet those who will be helpful and nice to them.

Response: **Help us to love you and to love one another.**

[d] Families are in need of love: May we brighten our own families by cheerfulness and love.

Response: **Help us to love you and to love one another.**

[e] Many are distressed by relatives and friends who have mysteriously disappeared: May those missing and their families find comfort.

Response: **Help us to love you and to love one another.**

[f] [other prayers]

Response: **Help us to love you and to love one another.**

[g] Our Father (perhaps sung)

11 Blessing

The grace of our Lord Jesus Christ, the love of God and the fellowship of the Holy Spirit be with us all. Amen.

12 Concluding song or music

"God loves you, God loves me."

From We are the Church: Music for primary Schools. Volume 1 (BRES tape) side 2, n.17 or

CFE		O&N
568	O Lord my God	404

Peace

1 Entrance music (tape or CD)

Choose a suitable piece of music or:

CFE		*O&N*
594	Peace is flowing like a river	442

2 Introduction

When Jews and Muslims greet one another they say "Peace" where we would say "Hello" or "Hi." Peace is very, very important for our country. We thank God for peace and we ask for peace for those in trouble.

3 Focus or symbol

– Cut-out of a dove, a gentle bird that symbolises peace.

4 Sign of the Cross

Jesus died that we might have peace. His Cross is the source of our peace, and so we begin "In the name of the Father and of the Son and of the Holy Spirit."

& 5 Hymn or song

CFE		*O&N*
595	Peace is flowing like a river	442
596	Peace is the gift	
597	Peace perfect peace	445

6 Reading

John 20:19-22 [paraphrased]

After Jesus died on the Cross, he rose and came to his disciples who had run away and let him down. He said "Peace be with you." They were filled with joy. Again He said "Peace be with you" and breathed on them saying "Receive the Holy Spirit."

7 Comment on reading

The source of our peace is Jesus who gives us the Holy Spirit. He asks us to give to others the peace he gives to us. We can work for peace, but in the end we must pray for it also. Peace is not something on its own: we cannot have a lasting peace except when we have justice, respect, love, generosity and forgiveness also. Because Jesus gives us peace, we should never be hurtful, or bully, or be cruel or unkind. A "peace person" wants to make other people happy.

8 Response to reading

To show that we want to be "peace persons" we offer a sign of peace, as we do at Mass, to the child or teacher near you.

Let us sing a song of peace for all here present and all we will remember today.

CFE		*O&N*
639	Shalom my friend	475

10 Thought-word-phrase for the day

I will try to be a peace-person today

9 Prayers

We turn to Jesus who said to his apostles, "I leave you peace, my peace I give you."

[a] We pray today for peace in the world especially in the North of Ireland, in the Holy Land and in..... [*name some place where there is unrest*]

Response: **Lord send us your peace**

[b] We pray for soldiers and police working with the United Nations keeping peace in Bosnia, Africa and in other places.

Response: **Lord send us your peace**

[c] We pray for neighbours who quarrel and for people who do not get on.

Response: **Lord send us your peace**

[d] We pray for all the families we represent that our homes will be places of peace.

Response: **Lord send us your peace**

[e] In silence we pray for anyone we may have had a row with in the past week.

Response: **Lord send us your peace**

[f] [other prayers]

Response: **Lord send us your peace**

[g] Our Father [perhaps sung]

11 Blessing

Numbers 6:24-26

May the Lord bless you and take care of you;
May the Lord be kind and gracious to you;
May the Lord look on you with favour and give you peace. Amen

12 Concluding music or song

CFE		*O&N*
478	Make me a channel of your peace	342

Corpus Christi – The Body of Christ

1 Entrance music (tape or CD) Choose a suitable piece of music or:

CFE 49 Among us and before us

2 Introduction

To day we give thanks for the Lord's most precious gift to the Church, the Eucharist, the Body and Blood of Christ, which is the main way in which Jesus brings us to his life and love. The sacrament has extraordinary power:

As we eat his Body which he gave for us, we grow in strength.
As we drink his blood which he poured our for us, we are washed clean.
(Roman Missal, Preface of Holy Eucharist I)

3 Focus or symbol

- Chalice and paten
- Picture/print/overhead of Last Supper
- Bread, water and wine and Missal

4 Sign of the Cross

The Cross is a constant reminder that Jesus opened his arms for each of us on Calvary, and so we begin, "In the name of the Father and of the Son and of the Holy Spirit."

5 Hymn or song

CFE		*O&N*
271/272	I am the bread of life	225/226
730	This is my body	556

6 Reading

John 6:51 paraphrase

Jesus said, "I am the living bread that came down from heaven. Those who eat this bread will live for ever. The bread that I will give them is my flesh, which I give so that the world may live."

7 Comment on reading

Our bodies need food, and so do our spiritual, inner selves. If we do not eat, then we will grow weak and eventually die. Not all foods are healthy. We need nourishing food. It is the same way with our souls, our inner selves. People try to feed their inner being with all kinds of escape, dangerous thoughts, and foolish distractions. But the real food that our inner being needs is God's Word and especially the Body of Jesus Christ who feeds us and makes us strong spiritually and holy. It is important that our lives match up to the gift we receive. At the end of Mass, the priest says, "Go in peace to love and serve the Lord." The Eucharist must lead us to love others as we have been loved by Jesus.

8 Response to reading

Pupils carry Eucharistic symbols to the front of the assembly, e.g. Bible, banner/poster, food for the poor, collection for some charity.

10 Thought-Word-Phrase for the day

"Christ be with me, wherever I go."
[prayer ascribed to St Patrick]

9 Prayers

We turn to Jesus and pray.

[a]	That we would grow to love the Mass and never take it for granted.
Response:	**Body of Christ save us.**
[b]	That priests and deacons will become holy as they celebrate the mysteries of the altar.
Response:	**Body of Christ save us.**
[c]	That those who are cut off from the Mass may know the love of Jesus.
Response:	**Body of Christ save us.**
[d]	That we may become one with other Christians separated from us in the Eucharist.
Response:	**Body of Christ save us.**
[e]	That we may always treasure the presence of Jesus on our altars.
Response:	**Body of Christ save us.**
[f]	[other prayers]
Response:	**Body of Christ save us.**
[g]	Our Father (perhaps sung)

11 Blessing

The grace of our Lord Jesus Christ, the love of God and the fellowship of the Holy Spirit be with us all. Amen.

12 Concluding song or music

CFE		*O&N*
106	Christ be beside me	79
663	Soul of my Saviour	498
	My Lord and my Master	361

The Holy Trinity

1 Entrance music (tape or CD)
Choose a suitable piece of music

2 Introduction

The feast of the Trinity is a celebration of love. Love begins in the Father; it is revealed to us in Jesus; it is poured out into our hearts through the Holy Spirit. We first encounter this love in our baptism; we grow in it through the Mass, Holy Communion, through good lives and through prayer.

3 Focus or symbol

- Rublev's icon of Trinity.
- Poster of Rembrandt's Prodigal Son.
- Overhead with attributes of God: e.g. creator, love, mercy, eternity, Father/Son/Spirit…

4 Sign of the Cross

The Trinity is the core of our faith and so we begin "In the name of the Father and of the Son and of the Holy Spirit."

5 Hymn or song

CFE		O&N
8	Abba, Father, send your Spirit	3
160	Father in my life I see	132

6 Reading *John 3:16 and Rom 8:14*

God loved the world so much that he gave his only Son so that everyone who believes in him may have eternal life. Those who are led by God's Spirit are children of God.

7 Comment on reading

The Holy Trinity is the family of God: God is revealed as Father, Son and Spirit. Father, because the first Person is in a sense the origin: from him comes the Son and the Spirit. But God is far beyond any goodness we can think of about human fathers. Indeed motherhood is sometimes used about God in the Bible (see *Catechism of the Catholic Church* # 239. God is neither man nor woman, but God is beyond all human thinking. The eternal God, Father, Son and Spirit decided from all eternity to create us. God also decided to redeem us and bring us into the family of God through baptism in the name of the Father, Son and Spirit. So our full identity or name is that we are "sons and daughters of the Father, brothers and sisters of Jesus Christ, temples or resting places of the Holy Spirit who is our Helper and Guide.

8 Response to reading

Sprinkle the assembly with holy water saying: "This water reminds us of our baptism in the name of the Father and of the Son and of the Holy Spirit." Some hymn mentioning the Trinity.

10 Thought Word-Phrase for the day

I am a member of the family of God

9 Prayers

As members of the family of God we pray.

[a] Holy Trinity, we thank you for the gift of baptism.
Response: **Glory be to the Father, and to the Son and to the Holy Spirit.**

[b] Loving God, bless all peoples and nations.
Response: **Glory be to the Father, and to the Son and to the Holy Spirit.**

[c] Jesus our Brother, help us to kind to others today.
Response: **Glory be to the Father, and to the Son and to the Holy Spirit.**

[d] Holy Spirit, Helper and Guide, give us the courage we need to be true to Jesus.
Response: **Glory be to the Father, and to the Son and to the Holy Spirit.**

[e] Holy Trinity, look in love on those who are searching for faith.
Response: **Glory be to the Father, and to the Son and to the Holy Spirit.**

[f] [other prayers]
Response: **Glory be to the Father, and to the Son and to the Holy Spirit.**

[g] Our Father (perhaps sung)

11 Blessing

The grace of our Lord Jesus Christ, the love of God and the fellowship of the Holy Spirit be with us all. Amen.

12 Concluding song or music

CFE		*O&N*
258	Holy, holy, holy, holy	214
	Praise to the Father	454

First Communion

1 Entrance music (tape or CD)

Choose a suitable piece of music

2 Introduction

We join with those who are preparing/have received their First Communion. We give thanks for this great gift from Jesus to those whom he loves.

3 Focus or symbol

- Copy of First Communion programme and a pupil's book.
- Poster of Mass/Eucharist/Last Supper.
- Overhead *"I am the bread of life."*

4 Sign of the Cross

The Cross reminds us that Jesus gave us the sacrament of Holy Communion on the night before he went to his death on the Cross. And so we begin "In the name of the Father and of the Son and of the Holy Spirit."

5 Hymn or song

CFE		*O&N*
271/272	I am the bread of life	225/226
578	One Bread, one Body	744

6 Reading

Mark 14:22-24

At the Last Supper while they were eating, Jesus took a piece of bread, gave a prayer of thanks, broke it, and gave it to his disciples. "Take it," he said, "this is my body." Then he took a cup, gave thanks to God, and handed it to them, and they all drank from it. Jesus said, "This is my blood which is poured out for many."

7 Comment on reading

When Jesus was going away, his disciples were sad. He found a way of being with them always through the sacrament of Holy Communion. In Holy Communion, and at Mass, we bring all our cares and worries to Jesus to find strength. At Mass too we offer ourselves and all the good we do for his glory. Mass, the Church teaches is "the source and the climax of the whole Christian life." We bring everything to it; we receive all the grace and strength we need from it. Holy Communion is the time when can most meet the love of Jesus: we get love from him; we tell him about our love for him; we pray for others in their need.

8 Response to reading

Children who are preparing for /have recently made their First Communion place symbols of their journey around the focus, e.g. religious object, Communion certificate.

10 Thought-Word-Phrase for the day

Jesus our Bread of Life

9 Prayers

We turn to Jesus the Bread of Life and pray.

[a] For all who have prepared us for this day.
Response: **I am the Bread of Life.**

[b] For more priests and deacons.
Response: **I am the Bread of Life.**

[c] For altar servers and ministers of the Eucharist.
Response: **I am the Bread of Life.**

[d] For all who have strayed from the Church.
Response: **I am the Bread of Life.**

[e] For a deep love and reverence for the Mass.
Response: **I am the Bread of Life.**

[f] [other prayers]
Response: **I am the Bread of Life.**

[g] Our Father (perhaps sung)

11 Blessing

May the blessing of Jesus, the Bread of Life come upon us this day;
May we draw closer to him in Holy Communion. Amen.

12 Concluding song or music

CFE		*O&N*
383	Lord Jesus Christ, you have come to us	326

Opening of the school year

1 Entrance music (tape or CD) Choose a suitable piece of music

2 Introduction

We gather to give thanks for the blessings that marked our school holidays and to ask the Lord's continuing blessing on this new school year. We welcome all our new pupils [and staff] who have joined this school community.
[We remember ________ who has/have died during the holidays.]

3 Focus or symbol

- School Mission statement.
- Candle and bible.
- Artefact/prayer/symbol of the patron/patroness of the school.

4 Sign of the Cross

The Cross is a reminder to all of us that Jesus who saved us, was called Teacher when he walked on this earth. We are joined with him in baptism and so we begin, "In the name of the Father and of the Son and of the Holy Spirit."

5 Hymn or song

CFE

576 On this *school* your blessing Lord

6 Reading

John 14: 23,26 (paraphrased)

Jesus said, "Those who love me will obey my teaching. My Father will love them, and my Father and I will come to them and live with them. The Helper, the Holy Spirit, whom the Father will send in my name, will teach you everything, and make you remember all that I have told you.

7 Comment on reading

Most people like new beginnings. It is nice to be back again at school, but the novelty will soon wear off. At the beginning of the year we look to what is central; in the life of our school which is summed up in our Mission Statement. School is very important, but it is not the only place where we are to learn: we learn at home too, not only by doing homework, but also from our family. That is the main place where we learn to be better people. At school there is much to be learned in the classroom. But the playground is also important. Here we learn how to play with others, how to be kind, how to enjoy ourselves without hurting others. In order to be fully alive as pupils and to develop, we need God's help at home, in the classroom and the playground. And so we ask for it. All of us need the help of God and so we pray for pupils, teachers, and staff. We look forward to a good year.

8 Response to reading

Attention is drawn to the Mission Statement, e.g. teachers come forward to receive copies of the Mission Statement;
e.g. new pupils are given a photocopy of Mission Statement to bring home;
e.g. the whole school reads aloud the Mission Statement.

10 Thought-Word-Phrase for the day

A new beginning

9 Prayers

We entrust this new school year to our loving God and pray.

[a] That all teachers, governors and parents may be blessed at this time.
Response: Lord, bless our school.

[b] That people who make decisions affecting our school may be generous and wise.
Response: Lord, bless our school.

[c] That new pupils and staff may be happy in this school.
Response: Lord, bless our school.

[d] That we may enjoy our learning and use our gifts and talents well.
Response: Lord, bless our school.

[e] That we may leave difficulties of the past year behind and begin in a new way to accept and forgive others.
Response: Lord, bless our school.

[f] [other prayers]
Response: Lord, bless our school.

[g] Our Father (perhaps sung)

11 Blessing

May the Lord bless us as we begin this new school year together.
May his loving presence surround us.
May we find peace and happiness in work and play. Amen.

12 Concluding song or music

CFE
832 On eagle's wings

Closing of the school year

1 Entrance music (tape or CD) Choose a suitable piece of music

2 Introduction

We gather to celebrate and give thanks for the many blessings we have received during this school year. We thank God for:

All the new knowledge we have gained.
All the new skills we have learned and developed.
All the friendships we have enjoyed.
All our successful moments.
All the difficulties that we thought were huge but which we got over in time and with patience.

We gather too to ask God's blessing on:

All our pupils leaving this school.
Teachers and staff who are leaving.
All of us that we will have a safe, refreshing and happy holiday time.

3 Focus or symbol

- School Mission Statement.
- Symbols of the year's achievement by school/class/group.
- Bible and candle.

4 Sign of the Cross

The Cross is a reminder that wherever we are we are joined to Jesus Christ by our baptism, and so we begin "In the name of the Father and of the Son and of the Holy Spirit."

5 Hymn or song

CFE		*O&N*
S11	One more step	
	Our God sent his son long ago	435

6 Reading

Isaiah 63: 7 and/or Matthew 13: 31-32

I will tell of the Lord's unfailing love;
I praise him for all he has done for us...

Jesus told them this parable: "The kingdom of heaven is like this. A man takes a mustard seed and sows it in his field. It is the smallest of all seeds, but when it grows up, it is the biggest of all plants. It becomes a tree so that birds come and make their nest in its branches."

7 Comment on reading

We are good at asking for what we need but we are not nearly so good at saying "thanks." This is a time to say "thank you" to God, to our teachers, to our fellow pupils and to our homes for the blessings of the past year. At the same time, we know that it was just one year; we still have much to learn and we have to be patient, like a farmer who must wait for the seed to grow into a plant.

But the year has surely taught us that troubles do pass. What worried us six months ago may be quite small now. The year has had difficult moments. We need to forgive as well as say thanks. Perhaps we need to say "sorry" also to some pupil or teacher, or member of school staff.

8 Response to reading

In the silence of our hearts we ask three questions:

Is there somebody I should say "sorry" to?
[silent pause]
Is there somebody I should forgive?
[silent pause]
What should I thank God and others for?
[silent pause]

10 Thought-Word-Phrase for the day

I have much to be thankful for

9 Prayers

We turn to God who loves us and give thanks:

[a]	That our school community may be blessed.
Response:	**Give thanks to the living God.**
[b]	That our teachers and all who have prepared us for this day may know your goodness.
Response:	**Give thanks to the living God.**
[c]	That we will bring the Good News that "Jesus is Lord" where ever we go.
Response:	**Give thanks to the living God.**
[d]	That we will have courage and strength to do always what is right.
Response:	**Give thanks to the living God.**
[e]	That we will use our gifts and talents for the good of others and the service of the Church.
Response:	**Give thanks to the living God.**
[f]	[other prayers]
Response:	**Give thanks to the living God.**
[g]	Our Father (perhaps sung)

11 Blessing

The grace of our Lord Jesus Christ, the love of God and the fellowship of the Holy Spirit be with us all. Amen.

12 Concluding song or music

CFE		*O&N*
189	Give thanks with a grateful heart	
512	Now thank we all our God	375

Welcome to new teachers or staff members

1 Entrance music (tape or CD) Choose a suitable piece of music

2 Introduction

Today we welcome a new teacher/staff member__________. We take the opportunity to pray for all our teachers and other staff that serve our school.

3 Focus or symbol

- School Mission Statement.
- Overhead with word "Welcome" (perhaps in various languages used by pupils, e.g.

  Willkommen,
  Bienvenu,
  Fáilte,
  Benvenuto
  [fem = Benvenuta],
  Welkom,
  Bienvenido
  [fem = Bienvenida]
  etc

4 Sign of the Cross

The Cross is at the heart of our Christian faith and a symbol of our Christian family, and so we begin "In the name of the Father and of the Son and of the Holy Spirit."

5 Hymn or song

CFE		*O&N*
486	May the peace of Christ be with you today	348
769	We are one in the Spirit	

6 Reading

1 Peter 4: 8-11 (paraphrased)

Above everything, love one another earnestly, because love covers over many sins. Open your homes to each other without complaining. We must all use for the good of others the special gifts we have received. We speak for God; we serve one another – in all things we seek the glory of God.

7 Comment on reading

Do you remember your first day at school when everything was so strange? Today we welcome ______________as teacher/staff member, we know that he/she will find our school strange. But settling in is more than knowing where the photocopier or the library are; it is much more a matter of being made feel at home, about being made welcome. A school is not a collection of individuals: it is a community, in some ways a family, in which we all have a contribution to make. Each of us has gifts that can enrich the school and make life here happier and better for others, teachers, staff and pupils.

8 Response to reading

New member of staff or teacher comes forward to receive from the Head Teacher the School Mission Statement, the Staff Handbook, and a bible.

10 Thought-Word-Phrase for the day

Our school is to be a family

9 Prayers

We lift up our school to the Lord.

[a] We pray that our school community may always reflect the values of Jesus Christ.
Response: **Lord hear us.**

[b] We pray that we may all co-operate for the benefit of the school.
Response: **Lord hear us.**

[c] We pray for ____________________ a new member of the school community, that he/she may be happy here.
Response: **Lord hear us.**

[d] We pray for those who have served in our school and have retired or moved elsewhere, that the Lord may be with them.
Response: **Lord hear us.**

[e] We pray for all whose lives we touch.
Response: **Lord hear us.**

[f] [other prayers]
Response: **Lord hear us.**

[g] Our Father (perhaps sung)

11 Blessing

Numbers 6: 24-26

May the Lord bless you and take care of you;
May the Lord be kind and gracious to you;
May the Lord look on you with favour and give you peace. Amen.

12 Concluding song or music

CFE		*O&N*
767	We are gathering together unto him	584

Retirement of teacher or staff member

1 Entrance music (tape or CD)

Choose a suitable piece of music

2 Introduction

As you know ____________________ is soon going to retire after many years of service in our school. We gather to give thanks for this dedicated service.

3 Focus or symbol

- Mission Statement.
- Candle.
- Overhead with *"Give thanks for __years of service."*
- Symbol of person: text book/office equipment etc.

4 Sign of the Cross

The Cross is central to the life and service of all Christians and so we begin "In the name of the Father and of the Son and of the Holy Spirit."

5 Hymn or song

CFE		*O&N*
189	Give thanks with a grateful heart	
	For you are my God	152

6 Reading

Romans 12:9-13

Love must be completely sincere. Hate what is evil, hold on to what is good. Love one another warmly as Christians, and be eager to show respect for one another. Work hard and do not be lazy. Serve the Lord with a heart full of devotion. Let your hope keep you joyful, be patient in your troubles and pray at all times. Share your belongings with your needy fellow Christians, and open your homes to strangers.

7 Comment on reading

We often hear it said that no person is an island. We are not independent, but depend on others. The school is a community in which each person has a place and a contribution to make. We need to appreciate what each person does. Today is an occasion to say thanks to ______________. But we should learn from this that perhaps we did not say "thanks" often enough. We say to our departing member "thanks," and "we will remember you."

8 Response to reading

Some presentation to the retiring person, e.g. flowers, a gift etc.

10 Thought-Word-Phrase for the day

We have so much to be thankful for

9 Prayers

We give thanks for the gifts we have received through__________

[a] May ________________ be rewarded for their contribution to our school.
Response: **Lord be gracious to us.**

[b] May ________________ have a happy and healthy retirement.
Response: **Lord be gracious to us.**

[c] May we all learn to co-operate and share our gifts with one another.
Response: **Lord be gracious to us.**

[d] May all past staff members and pupils of our school be blessed.
Response: **Lord be gracious to us.**

[e] May we always be good representatives of our school and witnesses to Jesus Christ.
Response: **Lord be gracious to us.**

[f] [other prayers]
Response: **Lord be gracious to us.**

[g] Our Father (perhaps sung)

11 Blessing

Numbers 6: 24-26

May the Lord bless you and take care of you;
May the Lord be kind and gracious to you;
May the Lord look on you with favour and give you peace. Amen.

12 Concluding song or music

CFE		*O&N*
639	Shalom, my friend	475

Harvest thanksgiving

1 Entrance music (tape or CD)
Choose a suitable piece of music

2 Introduction

We gather to give praise and thanks to the Lord for the gifts and the fruits of the earth. We remember also those who work and care for the earth, and those concerned for the environment.

3 Focus or symbol

- Overhead with *"Lord of the harvest we thank you."*
- Gardening/farming implement
- Sample of harvest: fruits, vegetables.

4 Sign of the Cross

We daily bless our food "In the name of the Father and of the Son and of the Holy Spirit."

5 Hymn or song

CFE		*O&N*
615	Reap me the earth	
306	In the earth the small seed is hidden	250
782	We plough the fields	597

6 Reading
Mark 4:26-29

Jesus went on to say, "The Kingdom of God is like this. A man scatters seed in his field. He sleeps at night, he is up and about during the day, and all the while the seeds are sprouting and growing. Yet he does not know how it happens. The soil itself makes the plants grow and bear fruit; first the tender stalk appears, then the ear, then the ear full of corn. When the corn is ripe, the man starts cutting it with his sickle, because harvest time has come.

7 Comment on reading

We take growth for granted, but it is such a mystery. Our lives depend on the earth being fruitful. But we need people who till the soil, who care for the earth, who deliver its produce to shops in the towns. We need to be thankful to so many people.

But we must also care for the earth. The Church teaches us respect for plants and for animals. We cannot abuse our world but must use it with care and prudence. We are to have a care not only for the rights of others, but also the rights of future generations. We think of the respect that the saints had for nature and animals like St. Francis Assisi. (See *Catechism of the Catholic Church* 2415-2418)

8 Response to reading

For a moment in silence we give thanks for the good gifts we have received.
(silent pause)
Pupils bring forward gifts of food for local needy people.

10 Thought-Word-Phrase for the day

The wonder and beauty of creation

9 Prayers

We give thanks to the Lord of the Harvest as we pray:

[a]	That the richer nations will have a concern for the poor and hungry of the world.
Response:	**All creation praise the Lord.**
[b]	That our politicians and the Christian community would always look after the poor in our midst.
Response:	**All creation praise the Lord.**
[c]	That farmers and traders would receive just payment for their labours.
Response:	**All creation praise the Lord.**
[d]	That we would always have respect for the earth and that wise policies be drawn up to protect our environment.
Response:	**All creation praise the Lord.**
[e]	That we would always have a deeper hunger for the things of God.
Response:	**All creation praise the Lord.**
[f]	[other prayers]
Response:	**All creation praise the Lord.**
[g]	Our Father (perhaps sung)

11 Blessing

Numbers 6: 24-26

May the Lord bless you and take care of you;
May the Lord be kind and gracious to you;
May the Lord look on you with favour and give you peace. Amen.

12 Concluding song or music

CFE		*O&N*
27	All things bright and beautiful	31

Inspection time

1 Entrance music (tape or CD) Choose a suitable piece of music

2 Introduction

We gather together to ask the Lord's blessing on our school during the coming Inspection. It is a time that is hard for everybody, and so we ask for grace and strength for one another, so that the Inspection may in its way be good for our school.

3 Focus or symbol

- School Mission Statement.
- Poster/banner/overhead with name of school patron/patroness.

4 Sign of the Cross

God who is One and Three is the centre of our school, and so we begin "In the name of the Father and of the Son and of the Holy Spirit."

5 Hymn or song

CFE		*O&N*
79	Shalom my friend	475
528	O God our help in ages past	392

6 Reading

1 Corinthians 4: 1-6 (paraphrased)

St. Paul wrote to the Corinthians: "Now, I am not at all concerned about being judged by you, or by any human standard; I don't even pass judgement on myself. My conscience is clear. But that does not prove that I am really all right. It is the Lord who passes judgement on me. Final judgement must wait on the Lord, who will bring to light everything, good and bad. Then all will receive from God the praise they deserve.

7 Comment on reading

Nobody likes inspections. But the government and the educational authorities who have responsibility, need to carry out inspections to see if things are going well and to give advice on how the school could be happier and a better place. So we try to be honest at the inspection so that the truth will come out of all the meetings, the discussions, the classes that are inspected. It is a time to pray especially for our head teacher and the teachers who find this a hard time.

But the reading we have heard from St. Paul reminds us that there is a judgement from God, which is even more important. God does not demand success from us; he does insist that we really try our best. The inspectors will make their report on our school, and we pray that it will be good. God will look at other matters like kindness, love. God would be much harder on bullies than on people not knowing their lessons. In this week we want to show off our school at its best; we want it also to be a school that Jesus Christ would be proud of.

8 Response to reading

The pupils look around at the teachers and say silently, "Bless us God in the coming week." The teachers look around at the pupils and say silently, "Bless us God in the coming week."

10 Thought-Word-Phrase for the day

These are difficult days:
let us be really,
really nice to each other

9 Prayers

The Holy Spirit is our Helper and Guide. We ask the blessing of the Spirit on our school.

[a] We pray for all the teachers.
Response: **Come Holy Spirit.**

[b] We pray for the Head Teacher and Deputy Head Teacher.
Response: **Come Holy Spirit.**

[c] We pray for all the pupils of our school.
Response: **Come Holy Spirit.**

[d] We pray for the school governors and for all who work in the school.
Response: **Come Holy Spirit.**

[e] We pray for the Inspectors.
Response: **Come Holy Spirit.**

[f] [other prayers]
Response: **Christ be beside us.**

[g] Our Father (perhaps sung)

11 Blessing

The grace of our Lord Jesus Christ, the love of God and the fellowship of the Holy Spirit be with us all. Amen.

12 Concluding song or music

CFE		*O&N*
388	Shine Jesus Shine	
693	The gift of the Holy Spirit	
A hymn invoking Holy Spirit		97–100

Examination time

1 Entrance music (tape or CD) Choose a suitable piece of music

2 Introduction

We come together to give thanks for the past year. We come also to pray for those doing examinations soon, that the Lord would give them peace in their hearts, wisdom in their study and a happy outcome of the examination.

3 Focus or symbol

- Candle
- Bible
- Textbooks

4 Sign of the Cross

The Cross reminds us of our Christian identity, and so we begin "In the name of the Father and of the Son and of the Holy Spirit."

5 Hymn or song

CFE		O&N
159	Father I place into your hands	133
633	Seek ye first the Kingdom of God	473

6 Reading *1 Peter 4:12-13; 3:15*

My dear friends, do not be surprised at the painful you are suffering as though something unusual were happening to you. Rather be glad that you are sharing Christ's sufferings, so that you may be full of joy when his glory is revealed. Have reverence for Christ in your hearts and honour him as Lord. Be ready at all times to answer anyone who ask you to explain the hope you have in you. But do it with gentleness and respect.

7 Comment on reading

None of us likes examinations. They are a trial, and there is always anxiety: Will I be able to answer the question? Will my memory fail? Suppose I panic? Our Christian faith gives us some advice that is helpful in this difficult time. We should pray for peace and calm so that we will be able to acquit ourselves to the best. We pray to the Holy Spirit for wisdom. Above all, we know that Jesus who went before us to the Cross will be with us. He knew anxiety about his death; he can strengthen us in our worry. But there is another Christian message that can be useful at examinations. An examination is not the end, even if we do not do as well as we expected. There is a deeper ground of hope and confidence than the knowledge we are bringing to the examination. That is, we are precious and loved by God, and God has a plan for us that in the end will turn out very well indeed.

8 Response to reading

Representatives of the examination class light candles to show that Christ is our light and our hope.

9 Prayers

We pray for the guidance of the Holy Spirit at this time.

[a] Spirit of wisdom, show us God's truth.
Response: Come Holy Spirit.

[b] Spirit of understanding, open our minds.
Response: Come Holy Spirit.

[c] Spirit of Right Judgement, help us to express our thoughts well.
Response: Come Holy Spirit.

[d] Spirit of Strength, protect us from discouragement.
Response: Come Holy Spirit.

[e] Spirit of Knowledge, be with us in our preparations.
Response: Come Holy Spirit.

[f] [other prayers]
Response: Come Holy Spirit.

[g] Our Father (perhaps sung)

10 Thought-Word-Phrase for the day

Come Holy Spirit

11 Blessing

The grace of our Lord Jesus Christ, the love of God and the fellowship of the Holy Spirit be with us all. Amen.

12 Concluding song or music

CFE		O&N
739	Though the mountains may fall	569

Remembrance [November]

1 Entrance music (tape or CD) Choose a suitable piece of music

2 Introduction

November is a time when we remember all the departed, especially family members and friends. It is also a time of national remembrance, when we recall those who have died for our country in wars, in the cause of peace in the North of Ireland, and with the United Nations and NATO forces.

3 Focus or symbol

- Poppy and candle

4 Sign of the Cross

The Cross is our hope – the dead will be raised by its power – and so we begin, "In the name of the Father and of the Son and of the Holy Spirit."

5 Hymn or song

CFE		O&N
271/272	I am the bread of life	225/b
513	Now the green blade riseth	
	The love I have for you, my Lord	536

6 Reading

Romans 14:7-8 (paraphrased)

We do not live for ourselves only; we do not die for ourselves only. If we live, it is for the Lord that we live, and if we die, it is for the lord that we die. So whether we live or die, we belong to the Lord.

7 Comment on reading

Remembrance Day is a time when as a nation we look back with gratitude to the countless men and women who died so that we might live in peace. The sign of this remembrance is the poppy, which grew abundantly in Flanders where thousands of soldiers died in World War I. The Monarch, the government, Church leaders and public representatives lead us in this remembrance. It is good that we remember people from our own area that have died during wars.

8 Response to reading

A procession of some children bearing names of local people who were members of the forces killed in action, names of deceased teachers or parish clergy, of friends and relations, and of parents who have died in the past year.

The names can be read out, or a chant such as the Taizé chant "Jesus, remember me" can be played or sung.

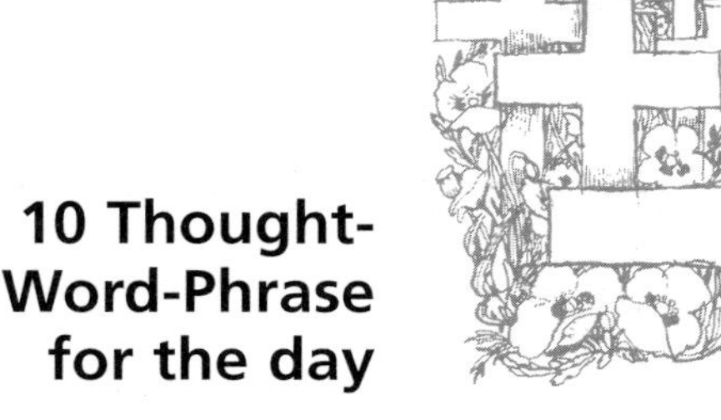

10 Thought-Word-Phrase for the day

"We will remember them"

9 Prayers

We now turn to our God in prayer.

[a] We give thanks for the lives of those who have died. We remember the good that they have done, and we recall with pride and gratitude the sacrifice of those who have died that others may have peace.
Response: **May the dead rest in peace, O Lord.**

[b] We commit all our loved ones to the Lord, and we hope one day to join them in eternal love.
Response: **May the dead rest in peace, O Lord**

[c] We pray for all who mourn, for all who have not come to terms with the fact of death, that they may be comforted by friends and by the grace of the Holy Spirit.
Response: **May the dead rest in peace, O Lord.**

[d] We remember in silence those who are dear to us. [*silent pause*].
Response: **May the dead rest in peace, O Lord.**

[e] [other prayers]
Response: **May the dead rest in peace, O Lord.**

Act of remembrance

They shall not grow old,
as we who are left grow old.
Age shall not weary them,
nor the years condemn.
At the going down of the sun
and in the morning,
We will remember them.

[f] Our Father (perhaps sung)

11 Blessing/prayer

Grant the dead eternal rest O Lord. Amen.
May they rest in peace. Amen.

12 Concluding song or music

CFE		O&N
369	Like a shepherd	727
706	The Lord's my shepherd	533
699	The King of Love	

Christian Unity [between 18 and 25 January]

1 Entrance music (tape or CD) Choose a suitable piece of music

2 Introduction

Jesus wanted all his disciples to be one; instead there are divisions between the Churches. There are big differences between Christians of the East and West, and between Catholics and Protestants in the West. These divisions have led to many wars and conflict: we think of the North of Ireland, of Yugoslavia and many other places. Since 1910 Christians have been working more to come together and to overcome envy and distrust. All over the world people pray this week for Christian unity.

3 Focus or symbol

- Crucifix and globe; or some artwork indicating division and unity.
- Poster/overhead with the names of the Christian Churches in the area.

4 Sign of the Cross

Though Christians are divided, they are united in Christ and in his Cross. And so we begin, "In the name of the Father and of the Son and of the Holy Spirit. Amen."

5 Hymn or song

CFE		*O&N*
732	This is my will	557
769	We are one in the Spirit	
	Ubi caritas	772

6 Reading

John 17:21-23

At the Last Supper Jesus prayed,
"I pray that they may all be one. Father! May they be in us, just as you are in me and I am in you. May they be one, so that the world may believe that you sent me. I gave them the glory you gave me, so that they may be one, just as you and I are one. I in them and you in me, so that they may be completely one, in order that the world may know that you sent me, and that you love them as you love me.

7 Comment on reading

Only about forty years ago there was a lot of bitterness and rivalry between the Churches. The pope and the leaders of other Churches have all decided that Christians should work for unity, so that there can be united witness to the world. In our area we have several Christian Churches (*specify*). We need to learn more about them and appreciate them, so that we can grow more together.

8 Response to reading

We think of the Churches in our area:

- The Church of England is the Established Church in England: it has a long tradition for worship and love of the scripture.
- The Methodist Church is known for the prayer life of its members and for their social concern.
- The Orthodox Churches have a very ancient worship and praise God with splendid liturgy.
- The Baptist Churches have put great emphasis on faith.
- The Pentecostal Churches pay special attention to the gifts of the Holy Spirit.
- The Salvation Army is known for their great work for those in need.
- The Congregational Churches have a fine sense of involvement of members in the running of the Church.
- The Catholic Church is rich in doctrine and sacraments, and in the guidance it gets from pope and bishops.
- The Society of Friends (Quakers) are known for their prayer life and their passion for peace.

Would it not be great if we could all share the gifts of the different Churches!

9 Prayers

We pray for the unity of all Christians:

[a] We pray that all Christians may be one in faith and love.
Response: **Lord, may we all be one.**

[b] We ask God for the grace of new life and holiness for all the Churches.
Response: **Lord, may we all be one.**

[c] We pray for the Queen and leaders of the Church of England.
Response: **Lord, may we all be one.**

[d] We remember all the Churches in our area:

The Church of England
The Methodist Church
The Congregational Churches,
The Orthodox Church
The Baptist Church
The Pentecostal Churches [*give name if known* e.g. Elim, Assembly of God, etc.]
The Society of Friends (Quakers)
The Salvation Army
Name any others in the area.

Response: **Lord, may we all be one.**

[e] We pray for those of other religions that they may always seek truth and find God in their lives. We remember Jews, Moslems, Sikhs, Buddhists, Hindus (*name others in area*). We remember those of no religion and those who seem to have lost faith.
Response: **Lord, may we all be one.**

[f] [other prayers]
Response: **Lord, may we all be one.**

[g] We say together the prayer that is common to all Christians:
Our Father… (perhaps sung)

10 Thought-Word-Phrase for the day

Division hurts,
unity builds and heals

11 Blessing

The grace of the Lord Jesus Christ, the love of God the Father and the fellowship of the Holy Spirit be with you all. Amen.

12 Concluding song or music

CFE		*O&N*
249	He's got the whole world in his hand	209
596	Peace is the gift	443
769	We are one in the Spirit	
	Peace I leave	440/441

Election time

1 Entrance music (tape or CD)
Choose a suitable piece of music

2 Introduction

Election time is very important for our country and our area. People go up for election because they think that they would be good people to serve the community. They think that their party is better than the others are. The Church does not support any party more than another; good people are found in all the parties. But we can pray that the outcome of the elections will be good for our people.

3 Focus or symbol

- National flag or flag/emblem of community.

4 Sign of the Cross

We are Christians praying about the coming elections. What we have in common with all Christians is holy baptism, and so we begin "In the name of the Father and of the Son and of the Holy Spirit."

5 Hymn or song

CFE		*O&N*
376	Look around you, can you see	316
567	O Lord, all the world belongs to you	403

6 Reading

Romans 13: 1-5 (paraphrased)

We all must obey state authorities because no authority exists without God's permission. Those who oppose the existing authority, oppose what God has ordered. Those who are in authority are not to be feared by those who do good, but by those who do evil. Would you like not to be afraid of those in authority? Then do what is good and they will praise you, because they are God's servants working for your good. You must obey the authorities as a matter of conscience.

7 Comment on reading

Election time. How much does it matter? It matters a lot, because good politicians can help our country and our area. The Church takes a very positive view of politics. We are told that it is our duty to vote, to take an interest in politics. "The Church praises and esteems those who devote themselves to the public good for the service of men and women and take upon themselves the burdens of public office...Citizens should cultivate a generous and loyal spirit of patriotism... Those with a talent for the difficult yet noble art of politics... should prepare themselves for it...and engage in political activity. They must dedicate themselves to the welfare of all." (Vatican II, *Church in the Modern World 75)*

8 Response to reading

Teacher holds up or waves election literature from all the parties, and says: "We pray that the right person will be elected."

10 Thought-Word-Phrase for the day

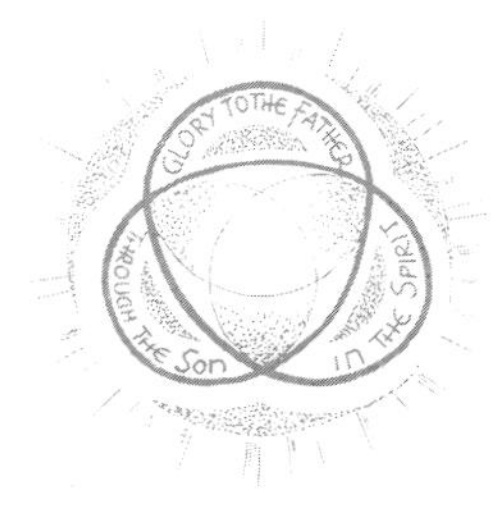

As we see election posters,
let us pray
"Lord bless our land"

9 Prayers

We pray for the political health of our country and area.

[a] We pray for those who vote that they may be wise when at the polling booth.
Response: **Lord bless our land.**

[b] We pray for all in public office that they may be unselfish and honest.
Response: **Lord bless our land.**

[c] We pray for the formation of a new government/local council.
Response: **Lord bless our land.**

In the case of by-elections:

We pray for the one who is to be our new representative.
Response: **Lord bless our land.**

[d] We pray for the media of TV, radio and newspapers that they report helpfully during the elections so that we shall be blessed by the results.
Response: **Lord bless our land.**

[e] We pray for those who do not become elected, that they will get over their disappointment.
Response: **Lord bless our land.**

[f] [other prayers]
Response: **Lord bless our land.**

[g] Our Father (perhaps sung)

11 Blessing

The grace of our Lord Jesus Christ, the love of God and the fellowship of the Holy Spirit be with us all. Amen.

12 Concluding song or music

CFE		O&N
249	He's got the whole world in his hand	209
478	Make me a channel of your peace	342

Anniversary of school's foundation

1 Entrance music (tape or CD) Choose a suitable piece of music

2 Introduction

We gather to give thanks for the ___________anniversary of our school. This is an opportunity to tell our story and to give thanks for all of the Lord's favour and blessing.

3 Focus or symbol

- Banner/overhead with words such as:

  Happy______Anniversary

  Date of Foundation

  Name of founder/first principal
- Historical documents
- Photographs
- Trophies, awards etc.

4 Sign of the Cross

The Cross is a constant reminder that Jesus is the reason why our school was founded in ______ and has continued to this day. So with gratitude we begin "In the name of the Father and of the Son and of the Holy Spirit."

5 Hymn or song

School hymn

CFE
576 On this *school* your blessing Lord

6 Reading *1 Corinthians 3: 9-11,16 (paraphrased)*

You are God's building. People must be careful how they build. God has already placed Jesus Christ as the one and only foundation, and no other foundation can be laid. Surely you know that you are God's temple and that God's Spirit lives in you.

7 Comment on reading

We celebrate the anniversary of our school. We reflect on the story of the school. We look back over the years since the foundation with thanksgiving. But the school we celebrate is not a building so much as people: pupils, teachers, parents and other staff: a school is something living. In the same way when we think of the Church we are not concerned with building but with people who are the temple, the home of the Holy Spirit. The centre of our school is people, but its foundation is Jesus Christ. He draws us into love; it is his doctrine that we live by; it is his way that we observe, by keeping the Commandments, especially the great Commandments of love.

8 Response to reading

The youngest and the eldest of the school pupils/or/a pupil and a teacher put in place some commemorative plaque, artefact, picture, scroll, poster etc.

10 Thought-Word-Phrase for the day

So much to be thankful for

9 Prayers

With thanksgiving we pray:

[a] That all whose generosity and good contributed to this school over the years may be blessed.
Response: **Lord bless our school.**

[b] That governors, teachers and parents will always work together for the good of this school.
Response: **Lord bless our school.**

[c] That Jesus Christ and his message may always be the centre of our school.
Response: **Lord bless our school.**

[d] That we may always have reason to be proud of our school.
Response: **Lord bless our school.**

[e] That all deceased members of our school community may have eternal life.
Response: **Lord bless our school.**

[f] [other prayers]
Response: **Lord bless our school.**

[g] Our Father (perhaps sung)

11 Blessing

May the Lord bless us and all that have helped to make this day possible. Amen.

12 Concluding song or music

CFE		*O&N*
194	Glorious God, King of creation	163
767	We are gathering together unto him	584
	We have come into his house	594

Ethnic celebrations

Note: This assembly is given in outline only. There is need for additions to focus on the particular people, ethnic group or event that is being celebrated.

1 Entrance music (tape or CD)

Choose a piece of music associated with group

2 Introduction

Our nation is multicultural, with peoples from all over the world being British and at home here.
Today we join with_______, who are celebrating _________________.
We pray for them and we thank God for the richness of cultures that make up modern Britain.

3 Focus or symbol

- Ethnic symbol
- Map with area of origin of ethnic group

4 Sign of the Cross

The Cross is salvation for all peoples, and so we begin "In the name of the Father and of the Son and of the Holy Spirit."

5 Hymn or song

Ethnic hymn *or*

CFE		*O&N*
22	All people that on earth do dwell	27

6 Reading

Isaiah 2: 2-3 (paraphrased)

In the days to come the mountain where the temple stands will be the highest one of all, towering above the hills. Many nations will come streaming to it, and their people will say, "Let us go up to the hill of the Lord. He will teach us what he wants us to do; we will walk in the paths that he has chosen.

7 Comment on reading

The Church teaches us that we are to respect and treasure the riches that belong to different peoples. We are to appreciate better the elements of truth and grace which are found among various peoples, and which are, as it were a secret presence of God." (*Catechism of the Catholic Church #856*, quoting Vatican II, *Missions 9* and *Church 17*). "Whatever goodness is found in people's hearts, or in particular customs and cultures, far from being lost are to be purified, and raised to a higher level,.. for the glory of God...and human happiness." (Vatican II, *Missions 9*). On the TV we are used to seeing different peoples, with different clothes, features, skin colour, hairstyles etc. We should be proud of our own ethnic background, and never be ashamed of our own people. We should treasure our culture: its music, its art, and its stories. But we must also welcome other cultures. The biggest task we have is to try to understand other cultures and races. Today as we join with the _____________ we try to appreciate their celebration.
[*Add some words about the ethnic celebration*]

8 Response to reading

Child brings up flowers to the ethnic symbol or pins a flower on the map indicating the place of ethnic origins.

10 Thought-Word-Phrase for the day

We are all different –
God loves us all

9 Prayers

We give thanks for the richness of our British society.

[a]	We pray for __________ who today celebrate __________
Response:	**You are Lord of all peoples.**
[b]	We pray for all the peoples who have settled here in Britain.
Response:	**You are Lord of all peoples.**
[c]	We pray for harmony and good race relations.
Response:	**You are Lord of all peoples.**
[d]	We pray for those who work for better race relations in our society.
Response:	**You are Lord of all peoples.**
[e]	We pray for refugees and immigrants.
Response:	**You are Lord of all peoples.**
[f]	[other prayers]
Response:	**You are Lord of all peoples.**
[g]	Our Father (perhaps sung)

11 Blessing

The grace of our Lord Jesus Christ, the love of God and the fellowship of the Holy Spirit be with us all. Amen.

12 Concluding song or music

Ethnic hymn or

CFE		*O&N*
24	All the earth proclaim the Lord	29

School outings–Journeys

1 Entrance music (tape or CD) Choose a suitable piece of music

2 Introduction

We gather and raise up to the Lord all who will; be going on the school outing this week to___________. We pray that they will have an enjoyable and safe time and that they will feel good after the trip. This journey is a reminder also to all of us about the need to be Christlike in our journeys, no matter how short.

3 Focus or symbol

- Candle
- Map or picture of destination of trip
- Picture of a church

4 Sign of the Cross

The Cross reminds us that life too is a journey, with our final destination being heaven, and so we begin "In the name of the Father and of the Son and of the Holy Spirit."

5 Hymn or song

CFE		O&N
765	Walk with me, O my Lord	582
S12	Walk in the light	547

6 Reading *John 4: 5-7 (paraphrased)*

Jesus came to a town in Samaria. Jesus, tired out by the journey sat down by a well. It was about noon. A Samaritan woman came to draw some water, and Jesus spoke to her and shared his love with her.

7 Comment on reading

It is always exciting to travel, to see new places and get new experiences. But there are some things, which are the same, wherever we go. Unless we travel to some very remote place, we shall always find a church, a place where God is worshipped. Again, even though the places we go to will be different, we will be the same, we will be Christians. There will always be opportunities to be kind and loving on a trip, perhaps especially on a trip when we get tired, or things seem to go wrong. Jesus was tired, but he still reached out to the local Samaritan woman who was in deep need. This teaches us to be attentive to one another during school trips. Part of this caring for others is of course a concern for safety on roads and in the things we do.

8 Response to reading

Representatives of the group which will be travelling come forward with names or literature/brochures about outing.

Group is sprinkled with Holy Water with the prayer, "May the Lord keep you safe."

10 Thought-Word-Phrase for the day

Jesus will be with us wherever we go

9 Prayers

We turn to Jesus in prayer.

[a] That all people travelling today may reach their destination safely.
Response: **Jesus you are the Way.**

[b] That drivers and other road-users may be careful and courteous.
Response: **Jesus you are the Way.**

[c] That rescue services and those concerned with traffic may be efficient and helpful.
Response: **Jesus you are the Way.**

[d] That people would have respect for those who are weak, infirm or with special needs.
Response: **Jesus you are the Way.**

[e] That the school outing may be safe and happy.
Response: **Jesus you are the Way.**

[f] [other prayers]
Response: **Jesus you are the Way.**

[g] Our Father (perhaps sung)

11 Blessing

The grace of our Lord Jesus Christ, the love of God and the fellowship of the Holy Spirit be with us all. Amen.

12 Concluding song or music

CFE		*O&N*
289	I will be with you	263
765	Walk with me, O my Lord	582

Death of a pupil

1 Entrance music (tape or CD) Choose a suitable piece of music

2 Introduction

In our distress and sorrow the one word that is surely coming to us all is "why?" There is no answer that will take away our pain. But there are answers that will give us strength. In our prayer today we remember ______________with thanksgiving our friend and pupil of this school. And we ask God's grace for ourselves.

3 Focus or symbol

- Overhead with words: *"The kingdom of heaven belongs to children,"* or *"Let the children come to me."*
- Photograph of deceased pupil or symbol of childhood, e.g. exercise book, school bag etc.

4 Sign of the Cross

______________ (*name*) was baptised into Christ with the sign of the Cross, and so we begin "In the name of the Father and of the Son and of the Holy Spirit."

5 Hymn or song

CFE		*O&N*
211	God who made the earth	
349	Lead me, guide me	
	The love I have for you	536

6 Reading

Isaiah 25:6-9 (paraphrased)

The Lord will prepare a great feast for all the nations on earth – a great meal with the riches food and drink. He will remove the cloud of sorrow hanging over us. He will wipe away all tears. Then we will say, "He is our God! We have put our trust in him and he has rescued us. He is the Lord. Now we are happy and joyful because he has saved us."

7 Comment on reading

The way we think about life and death will determine the consolation we receive in a time of sorrow. If we do not have a Christian vision, then the consolation we receive may be less. The Christian vision of death is of going home, going to Jesus, who has already gone to prepare a place for us. Therefore a good way of acting in times of sorrow is to trust in God as the reading has just told us. It means to give thanks for the life of the person we mourn. We recall with thanksgiving their friendship, their lives. We ask Jesus to look after them. At the same time it is a reminder to us that we sooner or later will die. And the way in which we live is our real preparation for death.

8 Response to reading

Representatives of the class of ___________ bring forward flowers, plants and light a candle.

10 Thought-Word-Phrase for the day

Our true home is in heaven

9 Prayers

We turn to our loving God and pray.

[a] That _________________ be safe in the presence of Jesus.
Response: **Remember us O Lord.**

[b] That the parents and relatives of ___________ may be strengthened at this time.
Response: **Remember us O Lord.**

[c] That all the friends of _________________ may be consoled at this time.
Response: **Remember us O Lord.**

[d] That all who nurse and care for the sick may be blessed.
Response: **Remember us O Lord.**

[e] That we all would live well and be ready to meet the Lord when he comes.
Response: **Remember us O Lord.**

[f] [other prayers]
Response: **Remember us O Lord.**

[g] Our Father (perhaps sung)

11 Blessing

The grace of our Lord Jesus Christ, the love of God and the fellowship of the Holy Spirit be with us all. Amen.

12 Concluding song or music

CFE		*O&N*
106	Christ be beside me	79
816	Yahweh, I know you are near	620
	Jesus, you are Lord	286

Death of a teacher / staff member / friend of school

1 Entrance music (tape or CD) Choose a suitable piece of music

2 Introduction

There are many ways of commemorating death. A common one is remembrance and thanksgiving. In our Catholic tradition we also pray that the dead person be at peace with God.

3 Focus or symbol

- Overhead with person's name and the words, *"Eternal rest."*
- Photograph/or articles associated with dead person.

4 Sign of the Cross

It is through our baptism that our greatest hope lies, and so we begin "In the name of the Father and of the Son and of the Holy Spirit."

5 Hymn or song

CFE		O&N
69	Be still and know that I am with you	57
369	Like a shepherd	727
543	O Lord, you are the centre of my life	

6 Reading

Wisdom 4:7-15 (paraphrased)

Even if they die before their time, good people will find rest. Life is not about how long we live, but how wisely we live. A good life is a long life. Good people try to please God, and God loves them. Coming to perfection in a short while is the same as having a long life. Good peoples' lives are pleasing to God. Foolish people never think that mercy and grace are what God has ready for good people. He will protect them.

7 Comment on reading

Our thoughts are very limited. Compared with God's wisdom, our thoughts are even foolish. God has a plan for each one of us. When we have done what he willed for us, when we have come into full life and goodness, God takes us to himself. God also has a care for those who remain. The way in which we fit into God's scheme of things is to live wisely. And we admit that we do not understand everything, much less the mystery of death. We treasure life, and we give thanks for the life of __________(*name*) who has enriched our school.

8 Response to reading

- A signed Mass card is placed at the focus for worship.
- A candle is lit.
- A flower or plant is laid.
- A copybook for signing condolences is placed for people to sign later.

10 Thought-Word-Phrase for the day

Jesus said,
"I am with you always."

9 Prayers

We turn to our living God and pray.

[a]	That ________________ may have eternal rest with the Lord.
Response:	**Jesus you are the resurrection and the Life.**
[b]	That ________________ may be rewarded for his/her contribution to this school.
Response:	**Jesus you are the resurrection and the Life.**
[c]	That the family, relatives and friends of ____________ may be consoled at this time.
Response:	**Jesus you are the resurrection and the Life.**
[d]	That all past members of this school who have left this world may be at peace with the Lord.
Response:	**Jesus you are the resurrection and the Life.**
[e]	That we may remember that we too are on a journey to the Father.
Response:	**Jesus you are the resurrection and the Life.**
[f]	[other prayers]
Response:	**Jesus you are the resurrection and the Life.**
[g]	Our Father (perhaps sung)

11 Blessing

To us who are alive may God give forgiveness;
To all who have died may God give light and peace. Amen.

12 Concluding song or music

CFE		*O&N*
40	Amazing grace	36
106	Christ be beside me	79

National grief

1 Entrance music (tape or CD)
Choose a suitable piece of music

2 Introduction

All over the country people are united in sorrow at the death of ______________
We join with them and commend those who mourn and our country to God.

3 Focus or symbol

- Candle
- Map of country
- Crucifix

4 Sign of the Cross

The Cross is a sign of hope even in distress, and so we begin "In the name of the Father and of the Son and of the Holy Spirit."

5 Hymn or song

CFE		O&N
9	Abide with me	4

6 Reading

Baruch 5: 1-4 (paraphrased)

The Lord said to his people: take off your clothes indicating sorrow and distress and put on instead for ever the beauty of God's glory. Put on the jewels of God's glory, for God means to show your beauty to other nations. God even gives you a new name: "Peace-through-Justice," "Glory through Fidelity." Get up, stand on the heights and turn your eyes towards the dawn. Be glad because God has remembered you.

7 Comment on reading

This reading was given to the prophet when there was national distress. The Bible never tells us to ignore suffering, or that suffering is not real. But God's word has two messages for those who are sad: he will be their strength; look beyond the present to God's future.

We mourn because of ______________. But we are not people without hope. We give thanks for the life of __________ and at the same time we look beyond the grave to where God is waiting for all his people. One day we shall all be one with him.

8 Response to reading

Hold up photo, emblem, of the dead person. Think of the good our country has gained from the life and achievements of the dead person. In silence give thanks.

10 Thought-Word-Phrase for the day

Lord, bless our nation

9 Prayers

We commend the dead and ourselves to God's grace and mercy.

[a] We pray that ______________ may be at peace with the Lord.
Response: **Our hope is all in you, Lord God.**

[b] We pray for our country united in sadness at this time.
Response: **Our hope is all in you, Lord God.**

[c] We pray for the family and those close to the one we mourn.
Response: **Our hope is all in you, Lord God.**

[d] We pray for all who have a role of leadership or authority in our country.
Response: **Our hope is all in you, Lord God.**

[e] We pray for ourselves on our pilgrim journey, inspired by the life of the one we grieve for.
Response: **Our hope is all in you, Lord God.**

[f] [other prayers]
Response: **Our hope is all in you, Lord God.**

[g] Our Father (perhaps sung)

11 Blessing

The grace of our Lord Jesus Christ, the love of God and the fellowship of the Holy Spirit be with us all. Amen.

12 Concluding song or music

CFE		*O&N*
705	The Lord's my shepherd	533/534
830	Be not afraid	627

A time of tragedy

1 Entrance music (tape or CD)

Choose a suitable piece of music

2 Introduction

We are all shocked by the tragic news that we saw on TV about____________________
We do not understand why such things can happen. Our response is to turn to God for strength and to ask his help and healing for those affected by the disaster.

3 Focus or symbol

- Candle
- Crucifix

4 Sign of the Cross

The Cross accompanies all of us through life. It is a source of strength and hope and so we begin, "In the name of the Father and of the Son and of the Holy Spirit."

5 Hymn or song

CFE		*O&N*
295	If God is for us	231
699	The King of love my shepherd is	528
	For to those who love God	149

6 Reading

Romans 8: 28-39 (selected verses)

We know that in all things God works for good with those who love him. In view of all this, what can we say? If God is for us, who can be against us? Certainly not God, who did not even keep back his own Son, but offered him for us all! I am certain that nothing can separate us from his love: neither death nor life, neither the present nor the future, nothing in world above nor the world below–there is nothing in all creation that will be able to separate us from the love of God which is ours through Jesus Christ our Lord.

7 Comment on reading

Jesus Christ came to save us and bring us life for ever. He did not take away all evil and suffering. Indeed he suffered terribly on the Cross. He even felt that God had abandoned him, but he managed to keep his faith and trust that in the Father's will all would be well. Jesus on the Cross said, "Into your hands I commend my spirit." God the Father was faithful and Jesus rose from the dead. As we think of the present tragedy, we place our hope in God who eventually will make things right in his Kingdom.

8 Response to reading

In silence think of those who are distressed and ask God to help them in their sorrow and difficulty.

10 Thought-Word-Phrase for the day

Our pains and difficulties are small compared with other people's

9 Prayers

We bring those in need to God.

[a] For those who suffer in the present tragedy.
Response: **Raise us up Lord.**

[b] For the relatives and friends of those involved.
Response: **Raise us up Lord.**

[c] For those who are helping and comforting at this time of disaster.
Response: **Raise us up Lord.**

[d] For the many people throughout the world who are in need and suffering at this time.
Response: **Raise us up Lord.**

[e] For ourselves that our hearts would be generous towards those in need.
Response: **Raise us up Lord.**

[f] [other prayers]
Response: **Raise us up Lord.**

[g] Our Father (perhaps sung)

11 Blessing

The grace of our Lord Jesus Christ, the love of God and the fellowship of the Holy Spirit be with us all. Amen.

12 Concluding song or music

CFE		*O&N*
69	Be still and know I am with you	57
830	Be not afraid	627

Reconciliation

1 Entrance music (tape or CD) Choose a suitable piece of music

2 Introduction

Some things are never finished. A floor that is swept today will have to be swept again soon. Clean hands do not stay clean. Lives are up and down. We live and associate with others: sometimes they annoy or even hurt us; sometimes we do the same to them. Relationships are always in need of building or rebuilding. The Christian words for this process are "reconciliation" which is from a Latin word meaning "calling together" or the word "atonement" which is three English words, "at-one-ment." We always need to get into a better relationship with God and with each other. Though there are certain times when there is more stress on reconciliation, such as family occasions, Christmas, or the Church seasons of Advent and Lent, we can say that any time can be a right time for mending relationships with God and with one another.

3 Focus or symbol

- Print of Rembrandt's Prodigal Son.

  or

- Overhead with words like *"Come back to me" "Love as I have loved you"* etc.

4 Sign of the Cross

The Cross is the sign of the costly love of God for us, which restored relationships through the death of his Son, and so we begin, "In the name of the Father and of the Son and of the Holy Spirit."

5 Hymn or song

"Water of Life, cleanse and refresh us" from *We are the Church. Music for Primary Schools.* (BRES tape). Vol. 1, side 2, number 7.
See also: CFE 401.

6 Reading

James 5:19 (paraphrased)

If a person should wander away from my love and another enable that person to return to my love, both will receive my blessing and forgiveness.

7 Comment on reading

Conversion and reconciliation both have the sense of turning back after having gone away. We hurt a friend, now we wish to come back and be friends again. Often too we need to turn back to God. The great way that he has provided is the sacrament of reconciliation. This sacrament has four names. It is the *Sacrament of Penance* because in it we bring to the Church the steps of conversion we make with God's grace or help. It is the *Sacrament of Confession* since in the sacrament we "confess" our sinfulness and we "confess" or proclaim God's mercy. It is the *Sacrament of Forgiveness* since by the priest's absolution we receive pardon and peace. It is the *Sacrament of Reconciliation* because it re-unites or reconciles us with God (see *Catechism of the Catholic Church*, art. 1423-1424). The meaning of the sacrament comes out in the words of absolution used by the priest:

> **God the Father of mercies, through the death and resurrection of his Son has reconciled us to himself and sent the Holy Spirit among us for the forgiveness of sins; through the ministry of the Church may God give you pardon and peace, and I absolve you from your sins in the name of the Father, and of the Son and of the Holy Spirit.** (art. 1449)

8 Response to reading

In the silence of our hearts we ask if there is something we ought to say "sorry" to God for, or if there is anybody we should say "sorry" to at this time.

10 Thought-Word-Phrase for the Day

Today I shall be quick to say "sorry."

9 Prayers

We pray for all who strive to lead people back to God, our loving Father.

[a] For the leaders of the Church, especially Pope______, and _________ our bishop.

Response: **Make our hearts new, O Lord.**

[b] For those who work for reconciliation, especially among different races.

Response: **Make our hearts new, O Lord.**

[c] For all who live in the darkness of anger and find it hard to forgive.

Response: **Make our hearts new, O Lord.**

[d] For anybody we may have hurt and for all who have hurt us.

Response: **Make our hearts new, O Lord.**

[e] For all who feel cut off and alone.

Response: **Make our hearts new, O Lord.**

[f] [other prayers]

Response: **Make our hearts new, O Lord.**

[g] Our Father (perhaps sung)

11 Blessing

May the Lord constantly bring us to himself, forgive our sinfulness and help us to help each other. Amen.

The grace of our Lord Jesus Christ, the love of God and the fellowship of the Holy Spirit be with us all. Amen.

12 Concluding song or music

CFE		*O&N*
347	Lay your hand gently upon us	295
369	Like a shepherd	727